Basic Geometry

Editors: Mary Dieterich and Sarah M. Anderson
Proofreader: Margaret Brown

COPYRIGHT © 2011 Mark Twain Media, Inc.

ISBN 978-1-58037-573-3

Printing No. CD-404154

Mark Twain Media, Inc., Publishers
Distributed by Carson-Dellosa Publishing LLC

Visit us at www.carsondellosa.com

Table of Contents

Table of Contents (cont.)

Introduction

Basic Geometry provides instruction and reinforcement exercises for the concepts that are the basis for all geometry. The students will be led from the fundamental notion of a point to rays, lines, planes, angles, transversals, two-dimensional shapes, and three-dimensional figures. Each concept builds on knowledge gained in previous sections.

The fundamental concepts of basic geometry are covered with text sections that explain each concept, process, or figure. Each concept is illustrated with easy-to-understand diagrams. Exercises are then provided for students to practice the skills they have learned. The step-by-step format facilitates instruction for the diverse learning styles and skill levels of middle-school students.

Topics covered include learning how to determine supplementary and complementary angles; identifying the relationships formed by adjacent angles, alternate interior angles, and vertical angles; and classification of triangles and quadrilaterals. Students will use a straight-edge and compass to create constructions of various geometric figures. Ultimately, students will experience three-dimensional objects and learn how to classify them, figure their volumes, and determine their surface areas. Patterns for foldable models are provided to give students opportunities for hands-on construction of several three-dimensional objects.

Basic Geometry addresses concepts covered in the National Council for Teachers of Mathematics (NCTM) Standards and supports Common Core State Standards (CCSS) for Mathematics. Correlations to state, national, and Canadian provincial standards may be found by visiting www.carsondellosa.com.

Points, Lines, and Planes

Introduction

Points and lines are the building blocks of geometry. Points, lines, planes, plane figures, and solids are abstract concepts. The pictures drawn on paper are models of these abstract concepts. For example, a straight mark made along the edge of a ruler is not a line, but a picture of part of a line. The mark made by the pencil of a compass is not a circle but a picture of a circle.

Drawings and constructions in geometry are representations of geometric ideas. They are not the ideas themselves. However, language tends to become monotonous when such directions as "draw a picture of a circle," "draw a model of a line," "draw a picture of a triangle," and so on, are used. For this reason, and because "draw" implies "picture," some authors merely say "draw a circle," "draw a line," "draw a triangle," and so on.

An important object of mathematics programs is to develop terminology and to present ideas in such a way that students will not have things to "unlearn" in later courses.

For example, color the circle and the rectangle below.

Did you color the inside of each figure, or did you merely trace the boundary? Is the center of a circle a point of the circle? Some agreement is needed as to what is meant by "rectangle" and by "circle." These two examples are intended to illustrate the reason why greater precision in language is necessary.

Undefined Terms

Points, lines, and planes are usually undefined terms in elementary and middle-school geometry. The definition of any given word in the dictionary is defined in terms of other words. If each of these words in turn is defined, eventually the original word will appear in one of the definitions. Hence the set of definitions is circular. In mathematics, such circularity is avoided by agreeing not to define certain terms.

Point

In modern geometry, a **point** is an undefined concept about which intuitive notions may be established. The tip of a needle when the needle is in a fixed location may represent a point in space. When the needle is moved, the tip suggests another point.

The tip of the needle may be moved, but not the mathematical point. A mathematical point is a fixed location. It cannot be moved.

A point may be represented by drawing a dot on paper. The dot, however, is not a mathematical point. It merely suggests a point. To distinguish different points represented by dots, capital letters are used. The five points represented by dots below are designated as A, B, C, D, and E. In this book, when a single capital letter is used, it will represent a point.

B •

D •

C •

E •

A •

Space may be considered as the set of all points or locations. In geometry, subsets of the set of points of space are considered. Examples of such subsets are a single point, the set of points in a line segment, and the set of points in a plane.

Line Segment

A **line segment** is a set of points. Imagine that the dotted line below is a picture of some of the points in a line segment. Then imagine that a point can be located between each two successive points and that this can be continued indefinitely. Between each pair of points, there is always another point.

Below are two points A and B. The dots and not the capital letters represent the points. (This is not always clear to children.) Use your ruler and make a straight mark to connect the two dots. Then imagine that this mark is the set of all points between A and B together with the points A and B.

A •   • B

The union of the two points A and B and the set of points between A and B is line segment AB. A line segment has two **endpoints**. The endpoints of segment AB are A and B. The symbol $\overline{AB}$ is used to designate this particular segment. The symbol $\overline{AB}$ is read as "line segment AB" or just "segment AB" for short. To name a line segment, two capital letters with a bar above them to suggest a segment are used.

Now make a second straight mark to connect points A and B above. How many straight marks can you make to connect these two points?

When a second mark is made from point A to point B, it is merely a retracing of the first mark. This suggests that one and only one segment can have A and B as endpoints. If the mark through A and B is extended to the edges of the paper, any other mark through A and B is merely a retracing of the first mark. The length of the mark is limited by the extent of the sheet of paper, but it is easy to imagine a mark that is unlimited in extent. This leads to the notion of a straight line.

Straight Line

A geometric **straight line** is unlimited in extent. It has no endpoints. A line is another undefined term in geometry, but a mark made along the edge of a ruler suggests the notion of a line. When the word *line* is used in this book, it will be understood to mean "straight line." A line is often represented as a double arrow, indicating that it extends without limit in both directions.

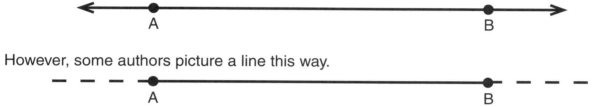

However, some authors picture a line this way.

To name a line, any two points in the line may first be selected and named by capital letters. For example, both lines pictured above may be named "line AB" or by the symbol $\overleftrightarrow{AB}$. The symbol $\overleftrightarrow{AB}$ is read "line AB." Notice that the double arrow above the two capital letters suggests one way of representing a line.

Relationships Between Points and Lines

Below is a single point Q. How many lines can be drawn through Q? Use your ruler to find the answer to this question. Lines that contain the same point are said to be **concurrent**.

●   Q

A single point may be contained in an unlimited number of lines.

If two lines intersect, they have only one point in common. In the illustration, the lines AB and CD intersect at a point E. $\overleftrightarrow{AB} \cap \overleftrightarrow{CD} = \{E\}$

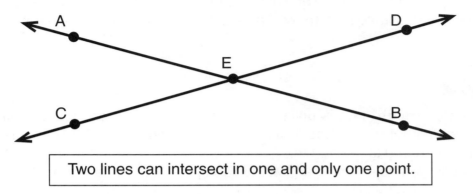

Two lines can intersect in one and only one point.

Two different points determine a line. Only one straight mark representing a line may be made through two dots representing points. Any other mark is a retracing of the first mark. That only one line contains the two distinct points A and B is illustrated below.

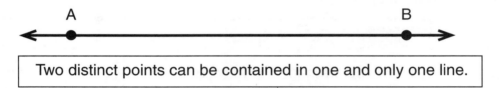

Two distinct points can be contained in one and only one line.

Collinear Points

If three points are located so that one is between the other two, the three points are said to be **collinear**. "Betweenness" is considered a property only of points in a line. Thus collinear points will always lie in a straight line. In the illustration A, B, and C lie in $\overleftrightarrow{AC}$ and represent collinear points. The point B is between A and C.

Three points not in the same straight line are said to be **noncollinear** points since there is no "betweenness" property. A, B, and C in the illustration below are noncollinear points. No point is between the other two. Notice that three noncollinear points determine three lines.

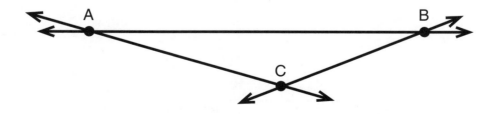

Ray

Any one point P in a line divides the set of points in the line into two half lines. Point P does not belong to either half line. In the illustration, the union of the point P and the set of points in the half line to the right of P is a set of points called a **ray**. Likewise, the union of P and all the points in the half line to the left of P is another set of points called a ray. A ray has only one endpoint.

To designate a ray, a second point of the ray may be named. The two rays pictured in the illustration below are named $\overrightarrow{OA}$ and $\overrightarrow{OB}$. The first capital letter names the one endpoint of the ray, and the second capital letter some other point on the ray. An arrow above two capital letters is the distinguishing symbol for a ray. The symbol $\overrightarrow{OA}$ is read "ray OA." (In later mathematics, this symbol, two capital letters with an arrow above them, may also be used to represent a vector.)

Each line contains an unlimited number of rays. In the illustration below, identify each of the following rays: $\overrightarrow{AE}$, $\overrightarrow{EA}$, $\overrightarrow{AB}$, $\overrightarrow{CA}$, $\overrightarrow{ED}$.

Notice that $\overrightarrow{AB}$ is the same ray as $\overrightarrow{AC}$, $\overrightarrow{AD}$, and $\overrightarrow{AE}$. Also notice that $\overrightarrow{ED}$ is the same ray as $\overrightarrow{EC}$, $\overrightarrow{EB}$, and $\overrightarrow{EA}$.

Plane

A **plane** is another undefined mathematical term. The set of points in a plane, like a point and the set of points in a line, has no physical existence. A plane is an abstract concept.

The flat surface of a table top suggests a portion of a plane. Imagine that the surface of the table top is extended in all directions. This imaginary unlimited flat surface may be considered as a representation of the set of points in a plane. Planes, like lines, are unlimited in extent. Other representations of parts of planes may include the walls, floor, and ceiling of a room.

Imagine all of the dots that could be made on a sheet of paper, and then imagine each dot as a point in a part of a plane. A plane is an unlimited set of points.

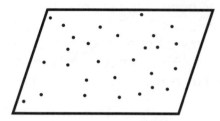

Next imagine all the different line segments that may be represented on the sheet of paper, and then imagine these segments as lines.

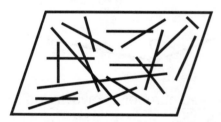

A plane contains an unlimited number of points, an unlimited number of line segments, an unlimited number of lines, an unlimited number of rays, and so on.

Usually a plane is represented as in the illustration and may be named in several different ways. It may be named by using one, two, three, or four letters or by a letter in a script font. In this discussion, a plane will be designated by a script letter. The plane illustrated may be designated as $\wp$.

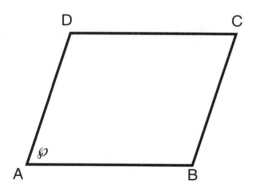

Relationships of Points, Lines, and Planes

Mark two dots A and B on a sheet of paper. Make a straight mark through the two dots. The mark may be thought of as a picture of a line in a plane. If any two different points in a plane are located, these two points determine a line. This suggest that:

> If two different points are in a plane, then the line determined by these points is in that same plane.

In other words, if two different points of a line are in a given plane, then the entire line is a subset of that plane. The illustration below shows a line AB in a plane $\Re$.

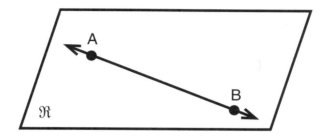

Two points are contained in an unlimited number of planes. Likewise, the line determined by these two points is contained in an unlimited number of planes. The illustration below represents three planes containing points A and B and hence $\overleftrightarrow{AB}$.

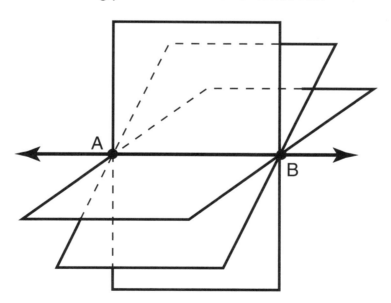

It is easy to imagine other planes containing A and B. This suggests that:

> An unlimited number of planes contain any two distinct points and the line determined by these two points.

A third relationship between points and a plane may be illustrated by spreading your thumb, index finger, and middle finger to support a book. The books rests firmly on the three fingers.

A three-legged stool does not wobble, while a badly made four-legged table will not stand firmly. Why? Three noncollinear points are always in the same plane, while four points may not all be in the same plane.

> Any three noncollinear points determine one and only one plane.

When the above property is assumed for a plane, two other relationships may be deduced.

Two intersecting lines determine a plane. Two points in one line and a third noncollinear point in the other line are three noncollinear points and thus determine a plane. In the following illustration, A, B, and C are three noncollinear points that determine a plane.

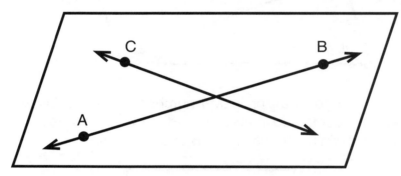

A line and a point not in that line determine a plane. Two different points in the same line and a third point not in that line are three noncollinear points and thus determine a plane. In the illustration, A and B are points in $\overleftrightarrow{AB}$, and C is a third point not collinear with A and B. The three noncollinear points determine a plane.

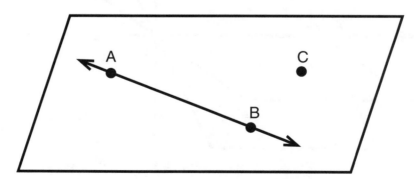

Coplanar Lines and Skew Lines

If two lines are in the same plane, they are called **coplanar** lines. Any two coplanar lines either intersect or are parallel. Conversely, if two lines are parallel or if they intersect, they are coplanar.

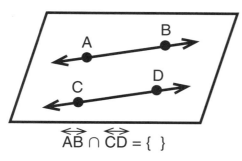

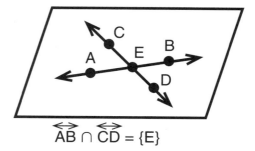

Parallel lines are coplanar lines that do not intersect. In set language, two coplanar lines are parallel if their intersection is the empty set.

Subsets of parallel lines are also said to be parallel. The following illustration shows two parallel segments, two parallel rays, and a line, a ray, and a line segment that are parallel.

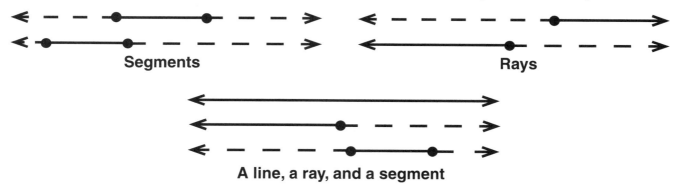

Two lines that are not coplanar are called **skew lines**. Such lines are neither parallel nor do they intersect. In the illustration below, $\overleftrightarrow{AB}$ and $\overleftrightarrow{CD}$ are skew lines.

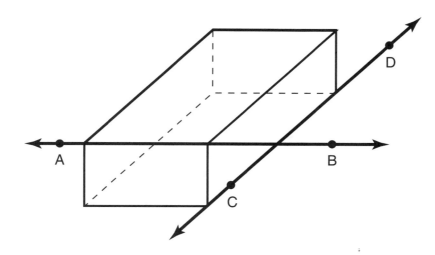

Intersections of Lines and Planes

Two planes either intersect or they are parallel. Two adjacent sidewalls of a room are representations of planes that intersect. The **intersection** of two planes is a line.

The intersection of two planes may also be represented by folding in halves a sheet of paper and creasing it sharply to make a tent. In the illustration below, $\overleftrightarrow{AB}$ is the line of intersection of the two planes.

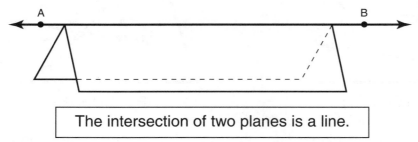

The intersection of two planes is a line.

Two planes that do not intersect are said to be **parallel**. In set language, two planes are parallel if their intersection is the empty set. In the illustration below, $\wp$ and $\Re$ are parallel planes. $\wp \cap \Re = \{\ \}$.

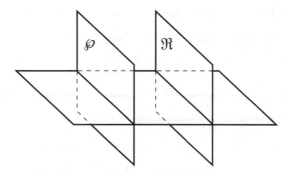

If a line intersects a plane, then either the line intersects the plane at one point or the whole line is a subset of the plane. The illustration on the left below show several lines, each with all of its points contained in the plane. The second illustration on the right below shows several lines, each intersecting the plane at a single point.

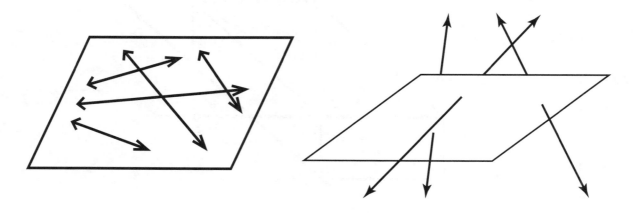

Angle

An **angle** is the set of points in the union of two rays with a common endpoint. Usually, it is stated that these two rays must not belong to the same line. This means that the angles considered in middle-school mathematics are acute, right, and obtuse angles.

In the illustration below, O is the endpoint of $\overrightarrow{OA}$, and O is the endpoint of $\overrightarrow{OB}$. The union of the two rays $\overrightarrow{OA}$ and $\overrightarrow{OB}$ is the angle AOB. Point O is the **vertex** of the angle and $\overrightarrow{OA}$ and $\overrightarrow{OB}$ are the **sides**. Angles may be named in several different ways. The angle illustrated may be named ∠AOB or ∠BOA. The symbol ∠ is read "angle." When three letters are used to name an angle, the letter designating the vertex is in the middle.

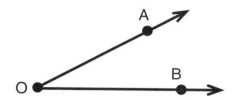

The angle may also be named ∠O. Notice that ∠O is not the same as O, which names a point.

Numerals are also used to name angles. In the illustrations below, the angles are designated as ∠A and ∠1.

An angle has an exterior and an interior. The **interior** is the set of points inside the angle, and the **exterior** is the set of points outside the angle. An angle separates a plane into three sets of points: the set of points in the exterior of the angle, the set of points in the angle, and the set of points in the interior of the angle.

In the following illustration of an angle ABC, the points G and O are in the interior of the angle, and the points M, U, and T are in the exterior of the angle. The points A, B, and C are points in the angle.

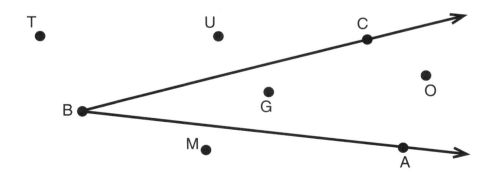

More precisely, the interior of an angle may be described as the intersection of sets of points. Ray BA is on line AB and ray BC is on line BC. Each line separates the plane into two half planes. The interior of Angle ABC is the intersection of the set of points in the half plane on the C side of line AB and the set of points in the half plane on the A side of line BC. The cross hatching in the illustration below represents the intersection of the two sets of points and, therefore, the interior of angle ABC.

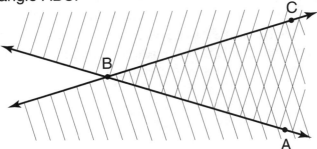

Polygon

A **polygon** is the union of the sets of points in three or more line segments. Each of the following is a polygon.

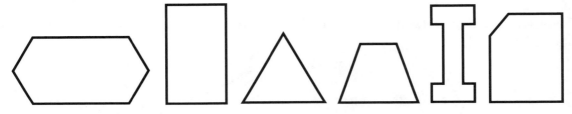

Triangle

The simplest polygon, which is the union of the sets of points in three line segments, is a **triangle**. The triangle represented below is the set of points in $\overline{AB} \cup \overline{BC} \cup \overline{CA}$. The triangle contains these points and only these points. No other points of the plane are in the triangle but are either in the interior or in the exterior of the triangle. $\overline{AB}$, $\overline{BC}$, and $\overline{CA}$ are sides of the triangle. A, B, and C are vertices (plural of vertex).

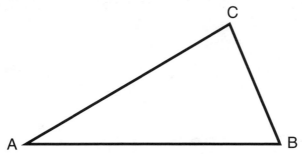

The angles associated with the triangle are ∠ABC, ∠BCA, and ∠CAB. These angles may also be designated as ∠B, ∠C, and ∠A. Does a triangle contain its angles? Remember that an angle is the union of two rays with a common endpoint.

Quadrilateral

A **quadrilateral** is a polygon that is the union of the sets of points in four line segments. Quadrilateral ABCD below is the set of points of $\overline{AB} \cup \overline{BC} \cup \overline{CD} \cup \overline{DA}$. The sides of the quadrilateral are $\overline{AB}$, $\overline{BC}$, $\overline{CD}$, and $\overline{DA}$. The vertices of the quadrilateral are A, B, C, and D.

The angles associated with the quadrilateral are ∠ABC, ∠BCD, ∠CDA, and ∠DAB. The angles may also be designated at ∠A, ∠B, ∠C, and ∠D. Does a quadrilateral contain its angles?

A quadrilateral with its opposite sides parallel is a **parallelogram**.

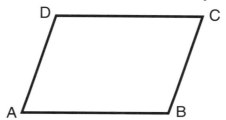

A quadrilateral with one and only one pair of parallel sides is a **trapezoid**.

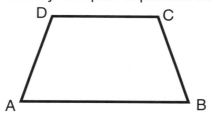

Other Polygons

A **pentagon** is a polygon that is the union of the sets of points in five line segments. Pentagon ABCDE below is the set of points of $\overline{AB} \cup \overline{BC} \cup \overline{CD} \cup \overline{DE} \cup \overline{EA}$.

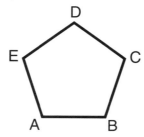

Polygons with more than five sides may be similarly defined. Those with six, seven, eight, nine, and ten sides are known, respectively, as **hexagons, heptagons, octagons, nonagons,** and **decagons.**

Polygonal Regions

A **polygonal region** is the union of the set of points in a polygon and the set of points in the interior of the polygon. The pictures below represent sets of points called polygonal regions.

 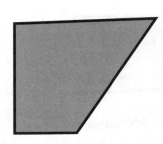  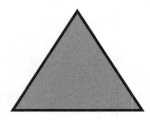

A polygon is a union of line segments and has only **length**. The region is a surface and has an **area**.

Symbols for Geometric Figures

Kind of Figure	How Named	How Drawn
1. Segment	$\overline{AB}$	A ●————————● B
2. Ray	$\overrightarrow{AB}$	A ●————————● B →
3. Line	$\overleftrightarrow{AB}$	← A ●————————● B →
4. Angle	∠ABC, ∠B, or ∠1	B, with rays to A and C

Name: _____ Date: _____

Points, Lines, and Planes: Exercises

1. Draw a line segment PQ. Then draw two other line segments that have Q as an endpoint.

2. Draw a line segment CD. Mark a point O between C and D. Draw a ray OK.

3. Dran an angle TOM. Mark Points C, A, and N inside the angle.

4. Draw a ray HI. Draw a segment HD.

5.

       R   A   Y

   a)   Three different names for the above line are _____, _____, and _____.

   b)   Three different segments on the above line are _____, _____, and _____.

   c)   Three different rays on the above line are _____, _____, and _____.

6. Draw lines AB, CD, and EF so that they are concurrent at a point K.

7. Draw a triangle SAM.

Name: _____   Date: _____

8.   Draw a quadrilateral JUDY.

9.   Draw a pentagon FRANK.

10. Draw a quadrilateral ABCD. Draw a triangle XYZ inside quadrilateral ABCD. Draw a pentagon MNOPQ outside the quadrilateral.

Find the following answers.

11.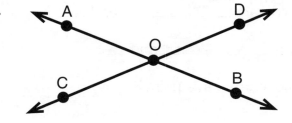

a) $\overleftrightarrow{AB} \cap \overleftrightarrow{CD}$ = _____

b) $\overrightarrow{OA} \cup \overrightarrow{OD}$ = _____

c) $\overrightarrow{OB} \cup \overrightarrow{OA}$ = _____

d) $\overline{OA} \cup \overline{OB}$ = _____

e) $\overrightarrow{OC} \cup \overrightarrow{OA}$ = _____

12.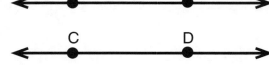

$\overleftrightarrow{AB}$ and $\overleftrightarrow{CD}$ are parallel lines.

$\overleftrightarrow{AB} \cap \overleftrightarrow{CD}$ = _____

Name: _____ Date: _____

Points, Lines, and Planes: Discovery Exercise

1. In the exercise that follows, the dots represent points in a plane. In each exercise, connect the dots in all possible ways by using a ruler and pencil. Before you draw the segments for each set of points, count the number of points and try to predict the number of possible segments. Then on the next page, record in the table the actual number of segments you drew.

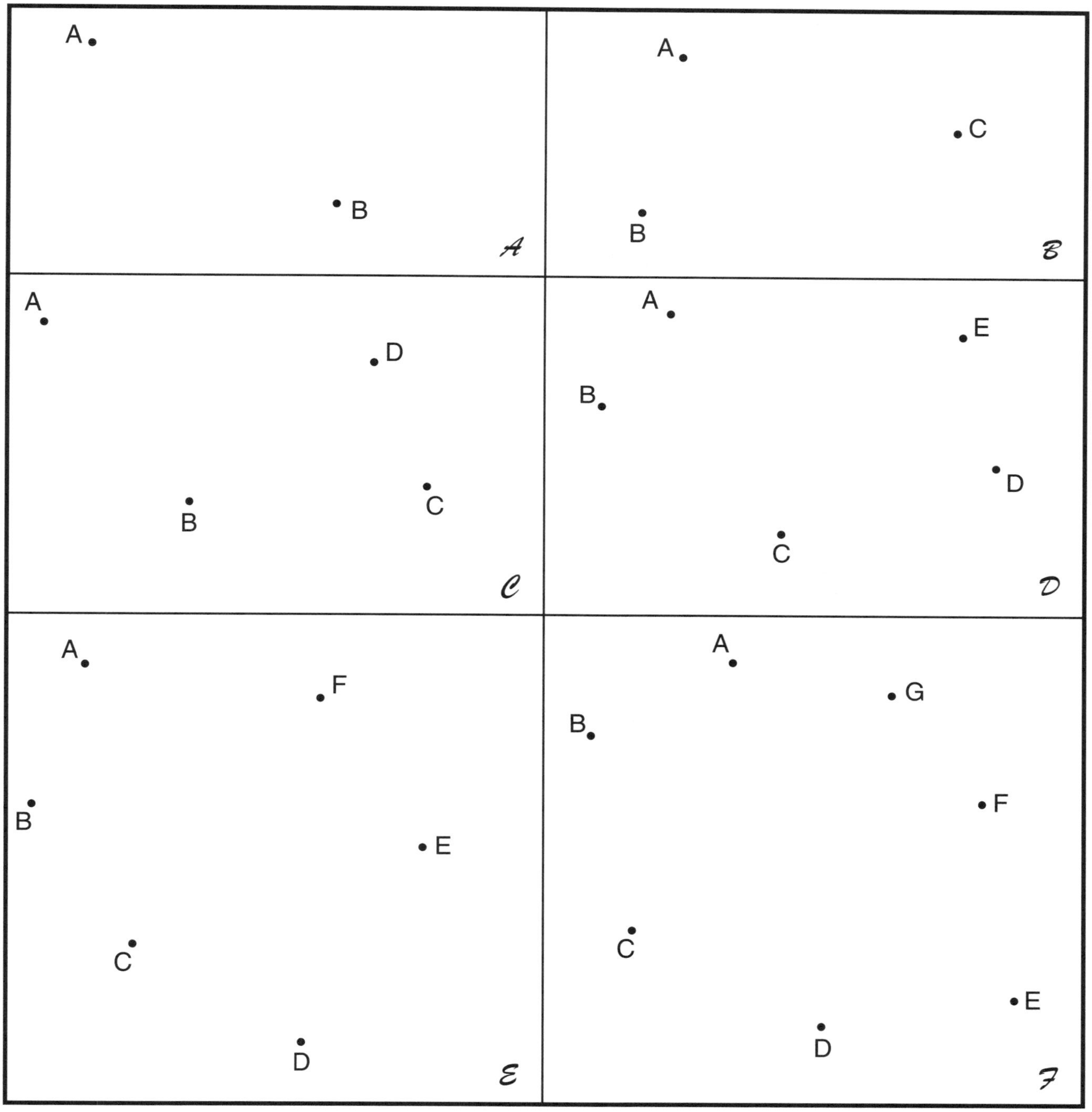

A•

•B

A

A•

•C

•
B

B

A•

•D

•
B

C•

C

A•

•E

B•

•D

•
C

D

A•

•F

•
B

•E

•
C

•
D

E

A•

•G

B•

•F

•
C

•
D

•E

F

Name: _____ Date: _____

2. After you complete the six exercises on the previous page, you may be able to discover a pattern. Use this pattern to find the number of possible segments when there are eight, nine, or ten points. Fill in the following chart with your findings.

Plane	Number of Points	Number of Segments
A	2	1
B	3	3
C	4	6
D	5	
E	6	
F	7	
	8	
	9	
	10	

3. Can you find a possible relationship between the number of points and the total number of segments? Write an equation for the relationship on the line below.

Let **p** represent the number of points.

Let **s** represent the number of segments.

s = _____

Name: _____ Date: _____

Congruence

Congruence Pre-Test Activities

1. Connect with lines the figures that have the same size and the same shape.

a)
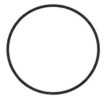

g)

b)
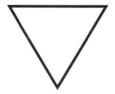

h)

c)
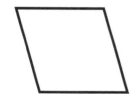

i)

d)

j)
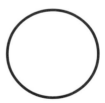

e)
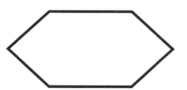

k)

f)
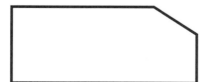

l)
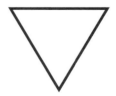

Name: _____ Date: _____

Congruence Pre-Test Activities (cont.)

2. Connect with lines the figures that have the same size and the same shape.

a)

b)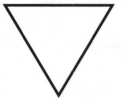

c)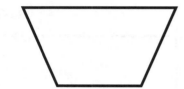

d)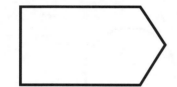

e)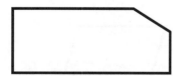

f)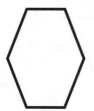

g)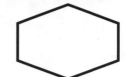

h)

i)

j)

k)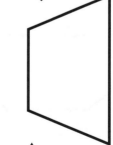

l)

Name: _____ Date: _____

Congruence Pre-Test Activities (cont.)

3. Trace segment AB on a thin sheet of paper. Then by placing the drawing over each of the other segments, determine which segments are the same length as segment AB. Circle those segments.

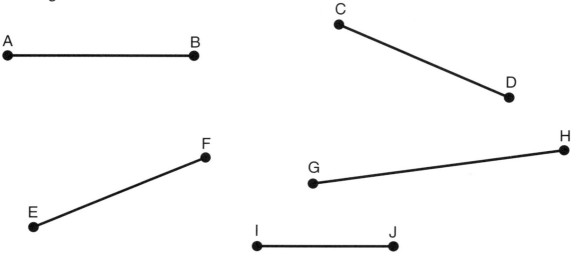

4. Trace angle ABC on a thin sheet of paper. Then by placing the drawing over each of the other angles, determine which angles are the same size as angle ABC. Circle those angles.

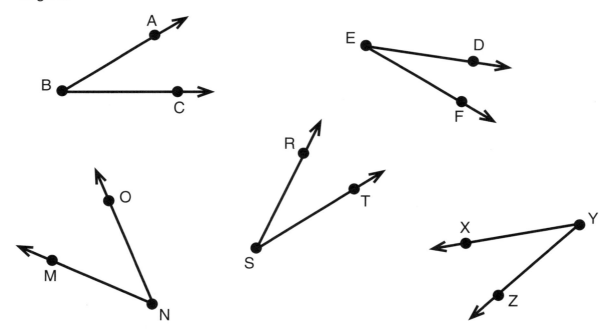

Name: _____ Date: _____

Congruence Pre-Test Activities (cont.)

5. Can you find pairs of figures that look as if a tracing of one of the figures would fit exactly on the other figure? Connect the mating figures with a line.

a)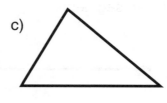

b)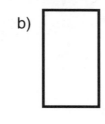

c)

d)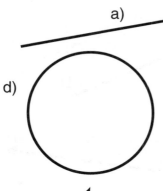

e)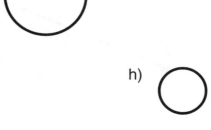

f)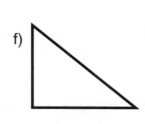

g)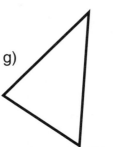

h)

i)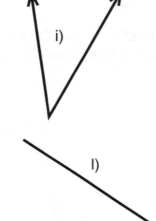

j)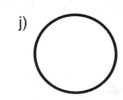

k)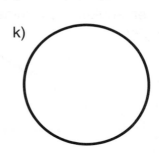

l)

m)

n)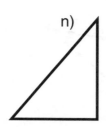

o)

p)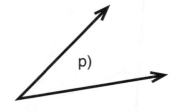

Congruence

None of the properties of geometric figures described in the preceding chapter depended upon the notion of size. However, the concept of size is basic to the definitions of such familiar figures as right angles, rectangles, squares, equilateral triangles, and so on.

Although geometric figures are abstract ideas, pictures and physical models are used to help develop important properties.

Two line segments, two angles, two closed plane curves, two plane regions, and so on are said to be **congruent** if they are exactly the same shape and size. Below are pictures of pairs of congruent figures.

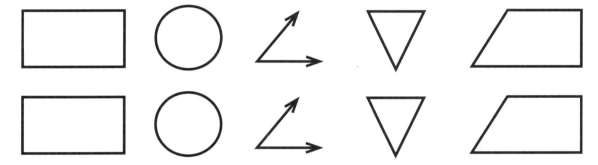

How can you show that the figures in each pair are congruent? Using thin paper, trace the figures in the lower row, and then place the traced figures over the corresponding ones in the upper row. Are the corresponding figures the same size and shape?

Congruence and Equality

In older texts, the word *equals* instead of *congruent* was used to state the relationship between line segments or between angles that had exactly the same size. The word **equals** is now widely accepted in mathematics to mean that two sets contain exactly the same elements or to mean that two numerals are names for the same number. These uses of equals are illustrated below.

Equality of sets: If A = {1, 2, 3} and B = {2, 1, 3}, then A = B.
Equality of numbers: 5 + 6 = 4 + 7

The word *congruent* is now used to state the relationship between two geometric figures that have the same size and shape. In the illustration below, $\overline{AB}$ is congruent to $\overline{CD}$.

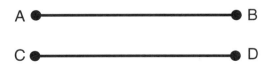

That $\overline{AB}$ is congruent to $\overline{CD}$ is written in symbols, $\overline{AB} \cong \overline{CD}$. The symbol $\cong$ is read "is congruent to."

Congruent Line Segments

Congruent line segments have the same length. $\overline{AB}$ and $\overline{CD}$ in the preceding illustration are representations of congruent line segments.

If a careful tracing of $\overline{AB}$ is made on thin paper and the tracing placed over $\overline{CD}$ so that A coincides with C, then B may be made to coincide with D.

Congruent Angles

Two angles may be congruent. In the illustration below, $\angle ABC$ is congruent to $\angle DEF$ ($\angle ABC \cong \angle DEF$).

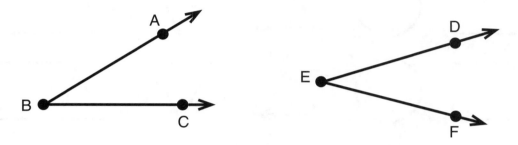

If a careful tracing of $\angle ABC$ is made on thin paper, and the tracing is placed over $\angle DEF$ so that B and E coincide, the tracing may be rotated so that the corresponding sides of the angles also lie on one another. This illustrates the meaning of the word *congruent* when it is applied to angles. All rays have the same length, regardless of how they are pictured.

Right Angles

When adjacent congruent angles are formed by a ray with an endpoint in a line (or by two lines), as in this diagram, the two angles are called **right angles**.

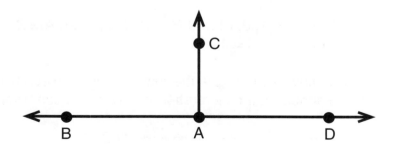

The two right angles in the diagram are $\angle BAC$ and $\angle CAD$. Also, $\overrightarrow{AC}$ is said to be **perpendicular** to $\overleftrightarrow{BD}$.

Classification of Triangles and Quadrilaterals

The notion of congruence for line segments and angles and the definition of a right angle make it possible to define and classify triangles and quadrilaterals.

1. Triangles
   a) A triangle is **equilateral** if its three sides are congruent.
   b) A triangle is **isosceles** if it has at least two congruent sides.
   c) A triangle is **scalene** if no two of its sides are congruent

| equilateral | isosceles | scalene |

   d) A triangle is **acute** if all of its angles are acute (less than 90 degrees).
   e) A triangle is **obtuse** if it has one obtuse angle (greater than 90 degrees).
   f) A triangle is a **right triangle** if it has one right angle (equal to 90 degrees).

 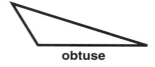

| acute | obtuse | right |

   g) A triangle is **equiangular** if all of its angles have the same measure.

equiangular

2. Quadrilaterals
   a) A **quadrilateral** is a polygon with four sides.
   b) A **parallelogram** is a quadrilateral with opposite sides parallel.
   c) A **rectangle** is a parallelogram with right angles.
   d) A **square** is a rectangle with adjacent sides congruent.
   e) A **rhombus** is a parallelogram with adjacent sizes congruent.
   f) A **trapezoid** is a quadrilateral with only one pair of parallel sides.

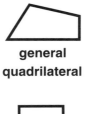 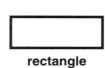

| general
quadrilateral | parallelogram | rectangle |

| square | rhombus | trapezoid |

Relationships of Quadrilaterals

The relationships of quadrilaterals may be illustrated by using a Venn diagram. If the universal set is the set of polygons:

1. the set of quadrilaterals is a subset of the set of polygons,
2. the set of parallelograms is a subset of the set of quadrilaterals,
3. the set of rectangles is a subset of the set of parallelograms,
4. the set of squares is a subset of the set of rectangles.

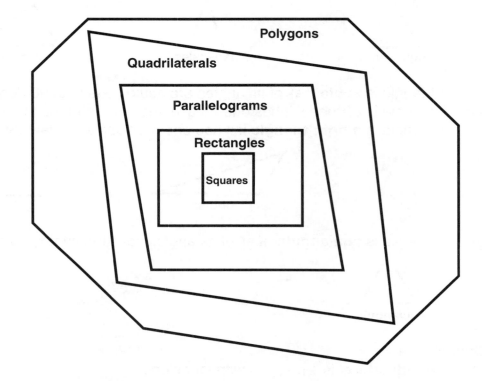

The Venn diagram may be helpful in writing definitions. A definition should name the thing to be defined, should classify it, and should give a distinguishing characteristic. Moreover, a properly stated definition is reversible.

Example: A square is a rectangle with adjacent sides congruent.

This definition may be reversed: A rectangle with adjacent sides congruent is a square.

Regular Polygons

A polygon is said to be **regular** if its sides are congruent and its angles are congruent. A **regular triangle** is an equilateral triangle. The three sides are congruent, and the three angles are congruent. A **regular quadrilateral** is a square. The four sides are congruent, and the four angles are congruent.

Some regular polygons are illustrated below.

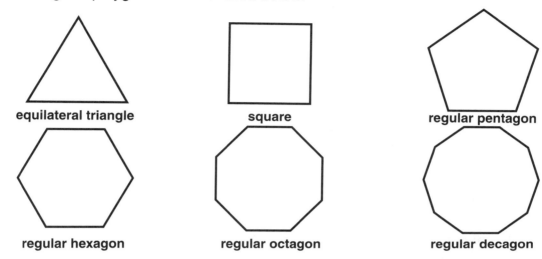

| equilateral triangle | square | regular pentagon |

| regular hexagon | regular octagon | regular decagon |

A circle will contain all of the vertices of a regular polygon.

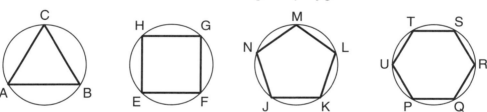

Circle

A **circle** is a closed plane curve with each point in the curve at the same distance from a given interior point called the **center**. The given distance from the center to a point on the circle is called the **radius** of the circle. The word *radius* may also refer to the segment joining the center with a point on the circle. In the illustration, the center of the circle is O. A and B represent two points on the circle. $\overline{OA}$ and $\overline{OB}$ represent radii (plural of radius) of the circle. All radii of a circle are congruent to one another. The circle illustrated may be designated as ⊙O, which is read "circle O."

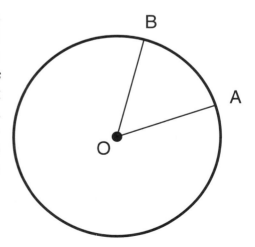

A **chord** is a line segment whose endpoints are points on the circle. In the illustration below, AB and CD represent chords.

A **diameter** is a chord whose endpoints are collinear with the center of a circle. The center is between the endpoints of the diameter. In the illustration, CD represents a diameter of the circle. All diameters of a circle are congruent to one another. Arcs CAD and CED are called **semicircles**.

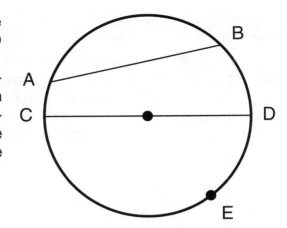

Arc

An arc is a part of a circle. A circle is a set of points; an **arc** is a subset of the set of points in a circle. In the illustration at right, the part of the picture of the circle drawn with a heavy line represents an arc. This arc may be named by using its endpoints and a point on the circle between the endpoints. In the illustration, the arc may be named arc AEB. This may be written in symbols as $\overset{\frown}{AEB}$. The symbol $\overset{\frown}{AEB}$ is read arc AEB. $\overset{\frown}{AEB}$ is classified as a **major arc**. An arc with only the two letters of its endpoints, such as $\overset{\frown}{AB}$, is classified as a **minor arc**. $\overset{\frown}{AB}$ is the heavy-lined area on the circle.

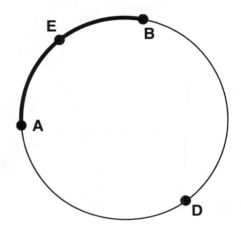

Symbols

Symbol	Meaning
⊙	circle
△	triangle
≅	is congruent to
↔	corresponds to
<	is less than
>	is greater than
$\overset{\frown}{AB}$	minor arc AB or arc AB
$\overset{\frown}{AEB}$	major arc AEB or arc AEB
⊥	is perpendicular to
∥	is parallel to

Name: _____ Date: _____

Congruence: Exercises

1. The dot marked A represents a given point in a plane. Use your ruler to locate 10 different points that are one inch from A.

                                    A •

    a)   What kind of pattern do the dots one inch from A seem to make?

         _____

    b)   Using A as a center, try to draw a picture of a circle through the points you located.

    c)   How was the notion of congruence used in locating these points?

         _____

         _____

2. How is the notion of congruence used in the measurement of length?

    _____

    _____

    a)   Find the measure of the long segment below in centimeters. _____

         ——— 1 cm   _____

    b)   Find the measure of the long segment below in inches. _____

         ——————— 1 in.   _____

3. How is the notion of congruence used in the measurement of area?

    _____

    _____

Name: _____ Date: _____

a) Find the measure of the area of this rectangular region in square centimeters.

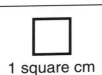 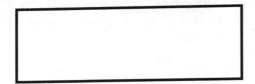

1 square cm

4. Examine the figures in each pair to determine whether they are congruent. Write "yes" if they are congruent or "no" if they are not congruent. In some cases, you may need to trace one of the figures and fit it over the other one in the pair to determine whether they are the same shape and size.

a) _____

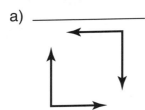

b) _____

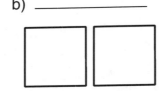

c) _____

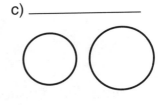

d) _____

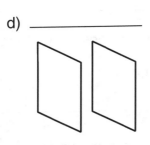

e) _____

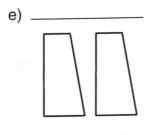

f) _____

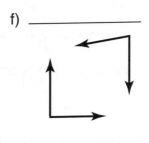

g) _____

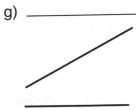

h) _____

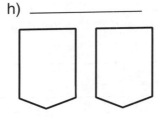

i) _____

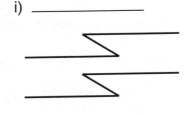

j) _____

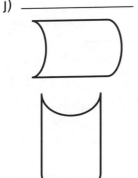

k) _____

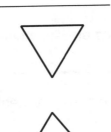

l) _____

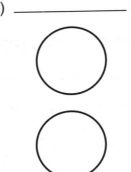

m) _____

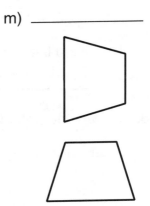

Name: _____ Date: _____

5. Draw a scalene right triangle.

6. Is it possible to draw an obtuse right triangle? If not, why?

_____

_____

7. Is an isosceles triangle also an equilateral triangle, or is an equilateral triangle also an isosceles triangle?

_____

_____

8. Measure the angles of an equilateral triangle. How else can you classify an equilateral triangle by the measurement of its angles?

_____

_____

9. Is a square always a rhombus? Is a rhombus always a square?

_____

_____

10. Is a parallelogram always a rectangle? Is a rectangle always a parallelogram?

_____

_____

11. How does a trapezoid differ from a parallelogram?

_____

_____

12. Is it possible for a quadrilateral to be a trapezoid and a parallelogram? Why or why not?

_____

_____

Name: _____ Date: _____

13. Slash marks and arcs are often used to denote the corresponding parts of congruent figures.

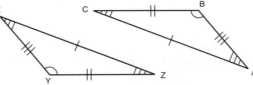

In the above triangles, the following parts correspond:

∠X ↔ ∠A   ∠Y ↔ ∠B   ∠Z ↔ ∠C

$\overline{XY}$ ↔ $\overline{AB}$ $\overline{YZ}$ ↔ $\overline{BC}$ $\overline{ZX}$ ↔ $\overline{CA}$

For any two congruent figures, order the letters representing the vertices so that the correspondence is indicated. In the above illustration, the order of the letters to indicate congruence of the triangles would be as follows.

△XYZ ≅ △ABC

a) For the two congruent triangles below, determine the corresponding angles and the corresponding sides.

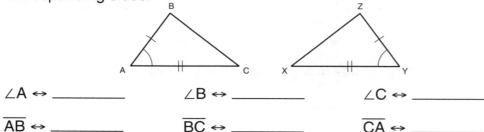

∠A ↔ _____   ∠B ↔ _____   ∠C ↔ _____

$\overline{AB}$ ↔ _____ $\overline{BC}$ ↔ _____ $\overline{CA}$ ↔ _____

Complete the sentence: △ABC ≅ _____

b) Repeat the above exercise with the pair of congruent quadrilaterals given below.

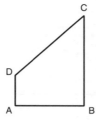 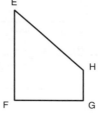

Name: _____ Date: _____

14. Sometimes appearances are deceiving. Examine each of the following illustrations and then answer the questions.

   a)   Are the vertical segments parallel? _____

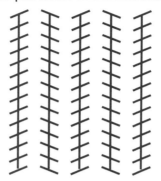

   b)   Are the two hexagonal shapes in the center of each group congruent? _____

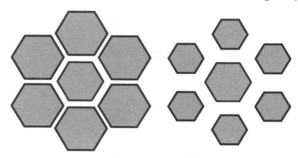

   c)   Which segments are congruent? Disregard the arrowheads. _____

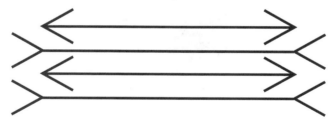

   d)   Look intently at the following figure for a few seconds. What do you see?

   _____

Name: _____ Date: _____

e)   Does the segment on the right belong to the same line as one of the segments on

the left? _____

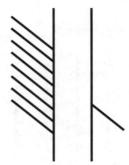

f)   What is the shape of the figure XYZ? _____

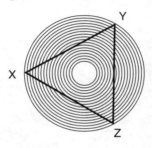

g)   Glance at this picture. What do you see? _____

_____

Now look intently at it again. What do you see? _____

_____

h)   Are AB and CD line segments or are they curved? _____

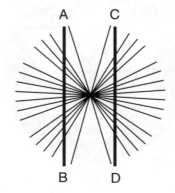

Congruence: Visual Aid for Geometry Activity

To help students understand the linear nature of polygons, a length of cord or heavy string is suggested as a geometry aid. With this, students can fashion triangles, quadrilaterals, pentagons, and so on.

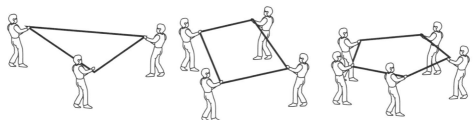

The cord becomes a more valuable tool for measurement and for the representation of the various kinds of triangles, quadrilaterals, and so on, if knots are tied at intervals of one foot.

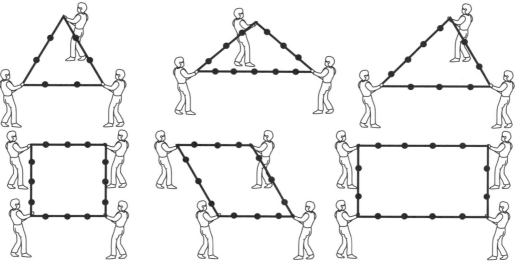

The linear nature of each figure, and consequently the linear nature of the perimeter, may be illustrated by forming the figure and then showing it as one long segment.

The perimeter of the square may be found in several different ways. A child may simply count the number of feet of cord it takes to make the figure. Another may see that since the length of each side is four feet, he or she can find the measure of the perimeter by addition: 4 + 4 + 4 + 4 = 16. The perimeter is 16 feet. Still another may discover that since the length of each side is 4, he or she can find the measure of the perimeter by multiplication: 4 x 4 = 16. The perimeter is 16 feet. From such observations, children can discover the meaning of the perimeter and can help develop formulas for the measures of the perimeters of various figures.

Congruence: Area Activity

The **area** of a triangle or quadrilateral can be found by knowing the lengths of the base of each figure and the height of each figure.

The area of a triangle is the same regardless of which classification of triangle you are dealing with. The area, **A**, is found by multiplying one-half times the length of the base of the triangle times the height of the triangle. **A = ½b x h**

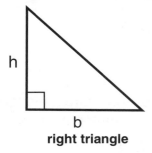 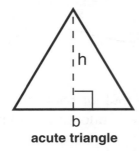 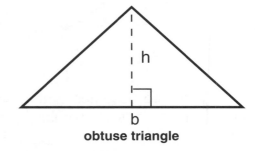

right triangle   **acute triangle**   **obtuse triangle**

The area of a quadrilateral depends on the particular classification of the quadrilateral. If it is a parallelogram, rectangle, square, or rhombus, the area, **A**, is found by multiplying the length of the base of the quadrilateral times the height of the quadrilateral. **A = b x h**

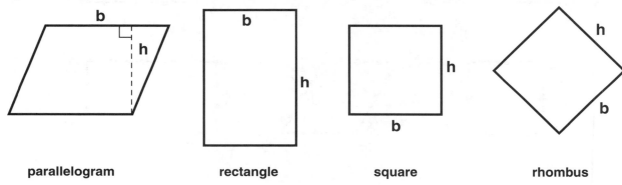

parallelogram   **rectangle**   **square**   **rhombus**

The area of a trapezoid is a little different. The area of a trapezoid depends on the lengths of the parallel sides and the height of the trapezoid (which is the distance between the parallel sides). The area, **A**, of a trapezoid is one-half of the sum of the lengths of the parallel sides (b_1 and b_2) times the height of the trapezoid. **A = ½(b_1 + b_2) x h**

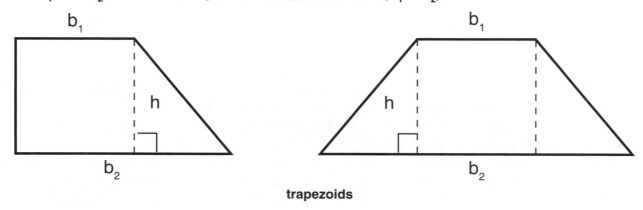

trapezoids

Name: _____ Date: _____

Find the area of the figures below.

1. _____

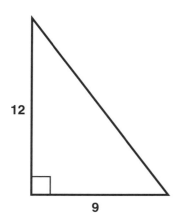

12

9

2. _____

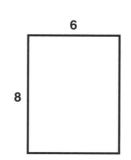

6

8

3. _____

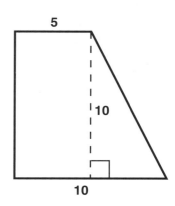

5

10

10

4. _____

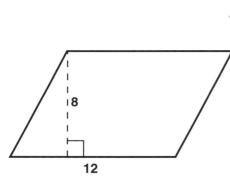

8

12

5. _____

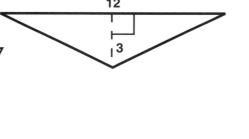

12

3

6. _____

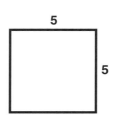

5

5

7. _____

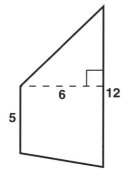

6   12

5

8. _____

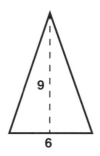

9

6

9. _____

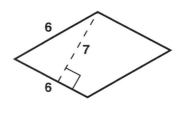

6

7

6

Convex and Concave Figures

Convex Figures

The points A and B located below belong to the set of points in the figure. Draw the segment that has A and B as endpoints.

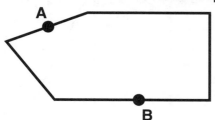

Do any of the points of the segment AB **in** the set of points belong to the figure itself?

Are any of the points of the segment AB **inside** the figure?

Are any of the points of the segment AB **outside** the figure?

Select any two distinct points A and B so that they are members of the set of points in the figure below. Try to select these points so that the segment AB goes outside the figure.

Select other points that are members of the set of points in the figure. Connect pairs of points. Can you find any segment that lies partly outside the figure?

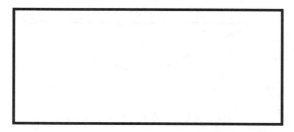

You should find that none of the segments go outside the figure. This is the distinguishing characteristic of a **convex figure**. If a line segment with endpoints in a simple closed figure contains no points in the exterior of the figure, the figure is a convex figure. The following are convex figures.

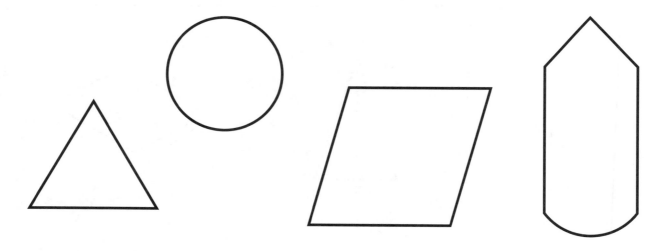

Concave Figures

The points A and B located below belong to the set of points in the figure. Draw the segment that has A and B as endpoints.

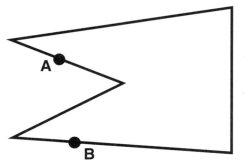

Are any of the points of the segment AB in the set of points **in** the figure?

Are any of the points of the segment AB **inside** the figure?

Are any of the points of the segment AB **outside** the figure?

Notice that a part of the segment AB is outside the figure. This is a characteristic of a **concave figure**. If two points can be chosen in a simple closed figure so that a line segment with these points as endpoints has points in the exterior of the figure, the figure is a concave figure. The following are concave figures.

Examples of Convex and Concave Figures

Convex

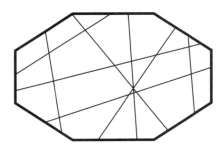

There are no line segments with points in the exterior of the figure.

Concave

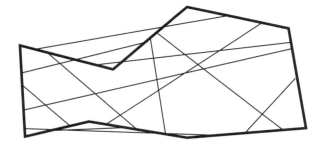

It is possible to draw line segments with points in the exterior of the figure.

Name: _____ Date: _____

Convex and Concave Figures: Exercises

1. Draw a convex quadrilateral and a concave quadrilateral.

2. Draw a concave hexagon, and then draw a convex pentagon inside it.

3. Draw a convex polygon with seven sides, and then draw a convex hexagon outside it.

4. Draw a concave pentagon inside a convex quadrilateral.

Lines of Symmetry

Fold a piece of paper in halves, cut out a design along the fold, and then open the paper. You will see two congruent shapes, one on each side of the fold.

   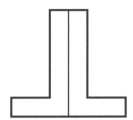

Fold another piece of paper and then place a drop of paint or colored glue on the inside along the fold. Press the paper firmly together to scatter the paint or glue. Again unfold the paper. Does the fold separate the paint or glue image into two congruent parts?

Line Symmetry

If a line through a plane figure is such that it separates the figure so that the part on one side is an exact reflection of the part on the other side, then the figure has **line symmetry**.

The notion of symmetry for plane figures involves the concepts of congruence and of a **reflection**, or mirror image. A line of symmetry must separate the figure into two congruent parts.

The figure below shows hexagon ABCDEF. $\overleftrightarrow{AD}$ is a line of symmetry. Trapezoid ABCD is congruent to trapezoid DEFA, and if you hold a mirror vertically along $\overleftrightarrow{AD}$, the part of the hexagon you can see, together with its reflection in the mirror, makes up the whole hexagon.

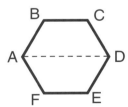

A line of symmetry not only separates the figure into two congruent parts, but it also separates the figure so that one of the parts can be placed exactly upon the other by reflecting one half of the figure in the line of symmetry. In other words, when you "fold the figure over the line of symmetry" the two halves fit together. If you fold a rectangle that is not a square over a diagonal, will the two triangles fall upon one another? Is the line along the diagonal a line of symmetry in this case?

Some figures have more than one line of symmetry.

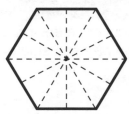

A rectangle that is not a square has two lines of symmetry.

An equilateral triangle has three lines of symmetry.

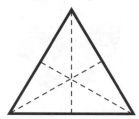

A circle has an unlimited number of lines of symmetry.

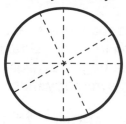

A square has four lines of symmetry.

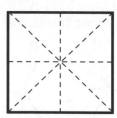

Some figures have no lines of symmetry.

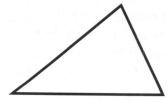

Name: _____ Date: _____

Lines of Symmetry: Exercises

1. How many lines of symmetry are in each letter of the following word?

GEOMETRY

___ ___ ___ ___ ___ ___ ___ ___

2. Fold a sheet of copy paper to determine the two lines of symmetry for that sheet of paper.

3. Fold a sheet of copy paper diagonally. Is the diagonal line a line of symmetry?

_____

4. How many lines of symmetry are there in each of these regular polygons?

a) _____   b) _____   c) _____   d) _____   e) _____

5. Draw the lines of symmetry of each of the following figures.

a)

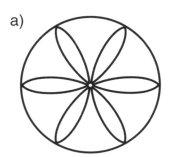

b)

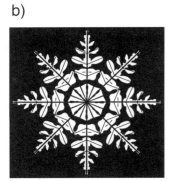

c)

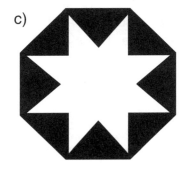

d)

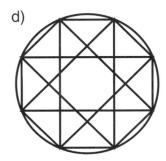

e)

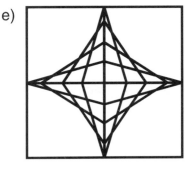

Name: _____ Date: _____

Measurement of Angles

Degrees

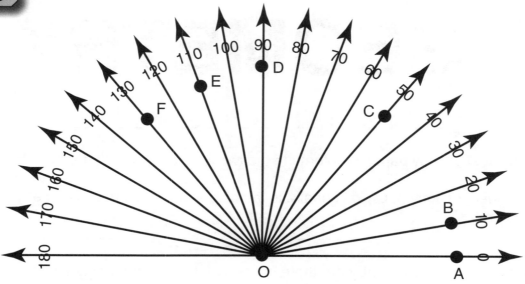

A basic concept in direct measurement is that the unit of measurement must be of the same nature as the thing to be measured. In the measurement of angles, the unit of measurement is an **angle of one degree**.

The number of degrees in an angle is called its **measure**. In the illustration above, the measure of angle AOB is 10. There are 10° in ∠AOB. The symbol for measure of an angle (in degrees), such as angle AOB, is **m ∠AOB = n** where **n** is a number representing the measure of the angle. The symbol m ∠AOB is read "the measure of angle AOB."

1. Use the illustration above to find the measures of the following angles.

    a)   m ∠AOC _____

    b)   m ∠AOD _____

    c)   m ∠AOE _____

    d)   m ∠AOF _____

    e)   m ∠BOC _____

    f)   m ∠COF _____

Name: _____ Date: _____

An angle may be measured with a protractor. Some protractors are marked in degrees with one scale that is read clockwise and another scale that is read counterclockwise. The sketch below shows a semicircular protractor placed on a set of rays with a common endpoint O. The base of the protractor is placed evenly on the line segment AH.

2. Find the measure in degrees of each angle designated below.

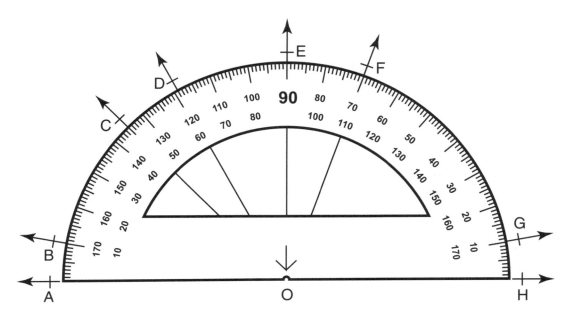

a)   m ∠AOB = _____

b)   m ∠AOE = _____

c)   m ∠GOH = _____

d)   m ∠FOA = _____

e)   m ∠DOA = _____

f)   m ∠COA = _____

g)   m ∠COD = _____
    Move a protractor so that the zero ray
    lies along $\overrightarrow{OC}$ (or $\overrightarrow{OD}$)

h)   m ∠FOG = _____
    Move a protractor so that the zero ray
    lies along $\overrightarrow{OG}$ (or $\overrightarrow{OF}$)

i)   m ∠COB = _____

j)   m ∠DOG = _____

k)   m ∠HOB = _____

Name: _____ Date: _____

Special Names for Angles According to Their Measures

An **acute angle** is an angle whose measure in degrees is less than 90. Verify by measuring each angle below that it is an acute angle.

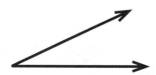 

A **right angle** is an angle whose measure in degrees is 90. Verify by measurement that the following represent right angles.

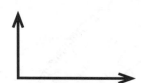

An **obtuse angle** is an angle whose measure in degrees is greater than 90 but less than 180. Verify by measurement that the following represent obtuse angles.

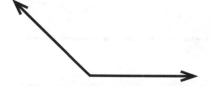 

Complementary and Supplementary Angles

Two angles are considered **complementary angles** if the sum of their angles is exactly 90 degrees. Two angles are considered **supplementary angles** if the sum of their angles is 180 degrees.

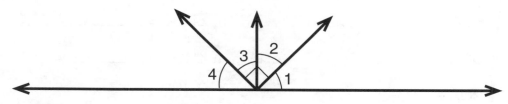

3. Which angles in the above diagram are complementary? _____

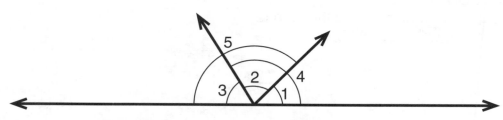

4. Which angles in the above diagram are supplementary? _____

Name: _____ Date: _____

Measurement of Angles: Exercises

1. Classify the following triangles:

    a) according to relative lengths of sides.

     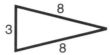

    _____   _____   _____

    b) according to the measures of the angles.

     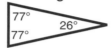 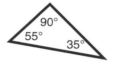

    _____   _____   _____

2. Several experiments may be used to help students discover that the sum of the measures of the angles of a plane triangle is the same for all triangles. Basic to this discovery is the knowledge of the sum of the measure in degrees of three angles such as those illustrated in the diagram below.

    a) $\overleftrightarrow{AB}$ is a straight line with P some point on $\overleftrightarrow{AB}$. Angles 1, 2, and 3 have the same vertex P. Use a protractor to measure the three angles.

    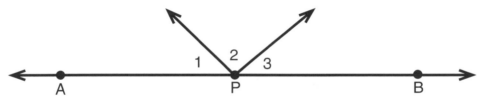

    The sum of the measures of the three angles is _____.

    b) Draw a triangle and cut it out. Then draw a line and select some point P on the line. Tear off the three vertices of the triangle and arrange them as illustrated with the vertices at P.

     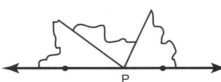

    What does this seem to demonstrate about the sum of the measures of the three angles of a triangle?

    _____

Name: _____ Date: _____

c) Draw a triangle ABC and cut it out.

Find the midpoint of $\overline{AC}$ and the midpoint of $\overline{BC}$. Draw the midsegment and fold the triangular region over the midsegment so that C falls on $\overline{AB}$. Fold again so that angles 1, 2, and 3 are in the position shown below.

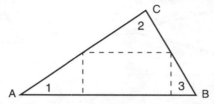 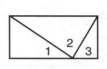

What does this seem to demonstrate about the sum of the measures of the three angles?

_____

d) Use a protractor to measure each angle of the triangles pictured below. Record the measures in the table and find the sum of the measures for each triangle.

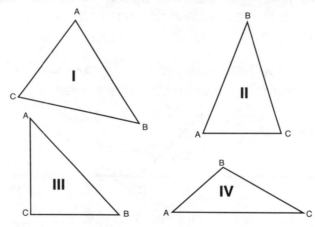

Angle	Triangle I	Triangle II	Triangle III	Triangle IV
∠A				
∠B				
∠C				
Sum				

What does the sum of the measures of the three angles for each triangle appear to be? _____

Now find the average of the four sums. The average is _____.

Name: _____ Date: _____

e)   △ABC is a triangle with a line XY through vertex C and parallel to base AB.

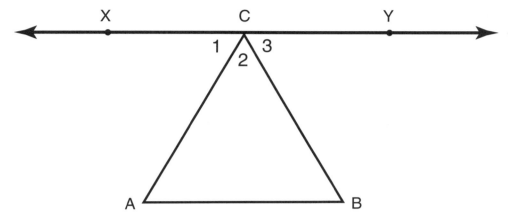

1)   What do you know about the sum of the measures in degrees of ∠1, ∠2, and ∠3?

_____

2)   Using your protractor, find the following measures.

m ∠A = _____   m ∠B = _____

m ∠1 = _____   m ∠3 = _____

3)   How do the measures of ∠A and ∠1 compare? _____

4)   How do the measures of ∠B and ∠3 compare? _____

5)   How does the sum of the measures of ∠1, ∠2, and ∠3 compare with the sum of the measures of ∠A, ∠B, and ∠2?

_____

3.   △ABC is an equilateral triangle. The three sides of an equilateral triangle are congruent. Measure each angle and record the information.

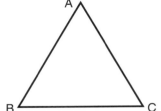

a)   m ∠A = _____

b)   m ∠B = _____

c)   m ∠C = _____

d)   What can you conclude about the three angles of an equilateral triangle?

_____

Name: _____ Date: _____

4. △ABC is an isosceles triangle. An isosceles triangle has at least two congruent sides. $\overline{AC}$ is congruent to $\overline{BC}$. Measure each angle and record the information.

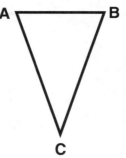

   a) m ∠A = _____

   b) m ∠B = _____

   c) m ∠C = _____

   d) What can you conclude about ∠A and ∠B?

   _____

5. △ABC is a scalene triangle. A scalene triangle has no congruent sides. Measure the sides (in inches) and the angles and record the information below.

   a) longest side _____

   b) next longest side _____

   c) shortest side _____

   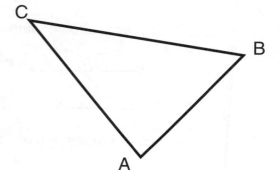

   d) largest angle _____

   e) next largest angle _____

   f) smallest angle _____

   g) What conclusions can you draw from this exercise?

   _____

   _____

   _____

   _____

Name: _____ Date: _____

6. The sum of the measures in degrees of the three angles of a triangle is 180. This information can be used to determine the sum of the measures of the angles of a polygon with any number of sides (without measurement). For each polygon that follows, draw all possible diagonals from vertex A. Assume all polygons to be regular (all sides with the same length and all angles congruent).

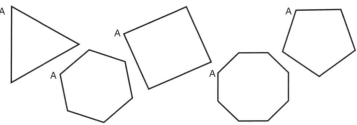

Complete the following table.

Number of sides	Number of angles	Number of diagonals	Number of triangles	Angle Sum of one triangle	Angle Sum of the polygon	Measure of each angle
3	3	0	1	180	180	60
4	4	1	2	180	360	90
5	5					
6						
7						
8						
9						
10						
11						
12						
n						

a) State a relationship between the number of sides of any polygon and the number of diagonals that can be drawn from one vertex.

_____

b) State a relationship between the number of sides of a polygon and the number of triangles formed by the sides and by the diagonals from one vertex.

_____

c) What is the sum of the measures of the three angles of one triangle?

_____

d) What is the sum of the measures of the interior angles of a polygon of n sides?

_____

Name: _____ Date: _____

7. $\overleftrightarrow{AB}$ and $\overleftrightarrow{CD}$ are a pair of parallel lines. $\overleftrightarrow{EF}$ is a line that intersects each of the parallel lines. $\overleftrightarrow{EF}$ is called a **transversal**.

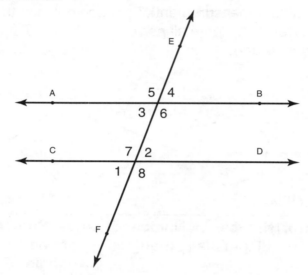

Use a protractor to measure each angle in the diagram above. Record the measures in the blanks below.

a)   m ∠1 = _____   e)   m ∠5 = _____

b)   m ∠2 = _____   f)   m ∠6 = _____

c)   m ∠3 = _____   g)   m ∠7 = _____

d)   m ∠4 = _____   h)   m ∠8 = _____

i)   Are angles with the same measure in degrees congruent?

_____, _____, _____, and _____ are congruent angles.

_____, _____, _____, and _____ are congruent angles.

j)   Use a color code to show the sets of congruent angles in the picture.

k)   What is the sum of the measures of angles 2 and 6? _____

l)   What is the sum of the measures of angles 3 and 7? _____

m)   What tentative conclusions can you draw about the sum of the measures of two interior angles on the same side of the transversal?

_____

Name: _____ Date: _____

When two parallel lines are cut by a transversal, eight angles are formed. Special names are given to these angles for convenience in discussing them.

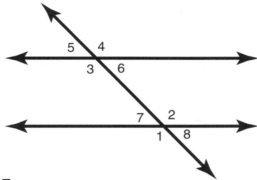

Interior angles: 2, 3, 6, and 7

Exterior angles: 1, 4, 5, and 8

Alternate interior angles: 2 and 3, 6 and 7

Alternate exterior angles: 5 and 8, 1 and 4

Corresponding angles: 1 and 3, 5 and 7, 2 and 4, 6 and 8

8. In the illustration below, line AB is parallel to line CD. Also, line EF is perpendicular to line CD.

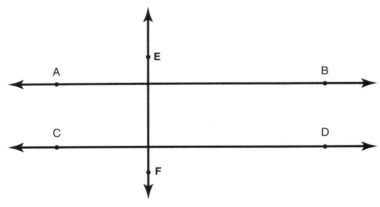

a)   What is the measure in degrees of each of the eight angles? _____

b)   Is line EF also perpendicular to line AB? _____

c)   If a line is perpendicular to one of two parallel lines, is it perpendicular to both of the

      parallel lines? _____

d)   Are two lines parallel if they are both perpendicular to the same line? _____

Name: _____ Date: _____

9. Four angles are associated with a pair of intersecting lines. In the illustration below, angles 1 and 2 are referred to as a pair of **vertical angles**, and angles 3 and 4 are also referred to as a pair of vertical angles.

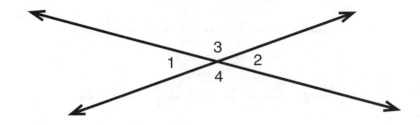

Use a protractor to measure each angle and record the information in the appropriate blanks.

a)   m ∠1 = _____   b)   m ∠2 = _____

c)   m ∠3 = _____   d)   m ∠4 = _____

e)   What appears to be true of a pair of vertical angles? _____

_____

10. In the figure below, angle 1 is referred to as an **exterior angle** of the triangle. Angles A and B are referred to as the two **nonadjacent interior angles** with reference to exterior angle 1. How are angles A and B related to 1?

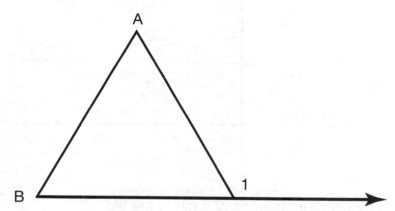

Find the measure of each of the following angles.

a)   m ∠A = _____   b)   m ∠B = _____   c)   m ∠1 = _____

The measure in degrees of an exterior angle of a triangle is equal to the sum of the measures of the two nonadjacent interior angles.

Name: _____ Date: _____

11. For each of the following figures, the number of degrees in one or more of the angles is given. Without measuring, find the number of degrees in each of the other angles. Write the degrees of each angle on the diagrams.

a)

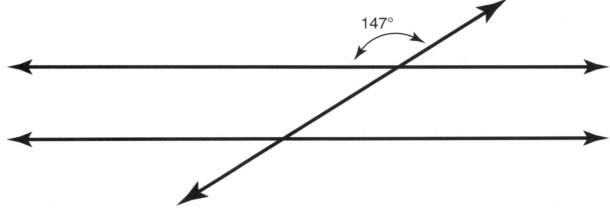

b)

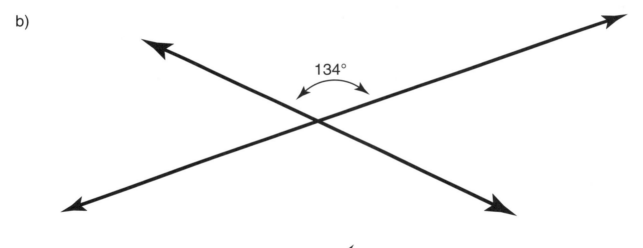

c)

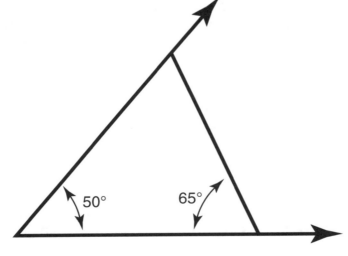

Name: _____ Date: _____

Constructions

Since the days of the ancient Greek philosopher Plato (380 B.C.), a clear distinction has been made between a drawing and a construction. Geometry, as practiced by the ancient Greeks, was much like a game, and to play the game, the players followed certain rules. One set of rules concerned the drawing instruments permitted in making constructions.

In a **construction**, points and lines were determined by using only two instruments, a straightedge (with no marking of any kind on it) and a compass.

The construction depended upon three assumptions:
1) two points determine a straight line.
2) all radii of the same circle are congruent.
3) radii of congruent circles are congruent.

In constructions, points are determined by the intersection of two circles, of two lines, or of a line and a circle. If two congruent circles intersect in two points, each of the points of intersection is the same distance from the centers of the two circles.

In the illustration below, circles A and B are congruent. They intersect in points C and D, each of which is the same distance from points A and B.

Why are $\overline{AC}$, $\overline{AD}$, $\overline{BC}$, and $\overline{BD}$ congruent? _____

_____

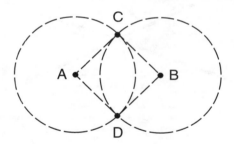

In the preceding illustration, the points C and D could have been located at equal distances from A and B by using intersecting arcs of congruent circles. The use of arcs to locate C and D is shown below. $\overline{AC}$, $\overline{AD}$, $\overline{BC}$, and $\overline{BD}$ are congruent segments because they are radii of congruent circles.

By making constructions to represent geometric ideas and by using measurements, students may be able to make interesting discoveries in Euclidean geometry.

Name: _____ Date: _____

Constructions: Intersection Exercises

1. In each of the following illustrations, label the point or points of intersection.

a)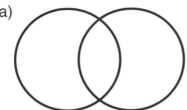

b)

c)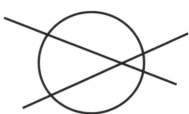

d)

e)

f)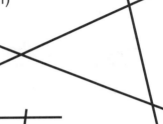

g)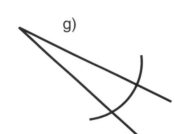

h)

i)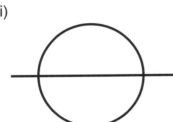

j)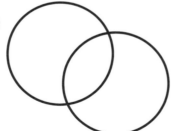

k)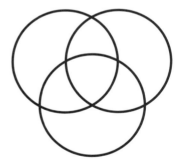

2. Draw each segment determined by the two points of intersection of the circles.

a)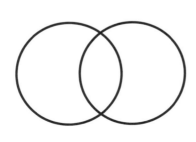

b)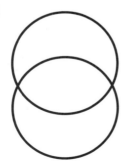

c)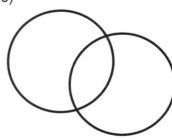

Name: _____ Date: _____

A. Construct a Line Segment Congruent to a Given Segment

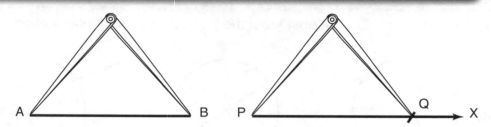

1. Let $\overline{AB}$ be the given segment.
2. Draw any ray PX.
3. With $\overline{AB}$ as radius and with P as center, draw an arc that intersects $\overrightarrow{PX}$ at Q.
4. $\overline{AB} \cong \overline{PQ}$.

Construct a Line Segment: Exercise

Use a compass to construct a segment that is three times the length of the segment RS.

B. Bisect a Line Segment

$\overline{AB}$ is a line segment. To **bisect** segment AB is to find its midpoint so that segment AB is divided into two congruent parts.

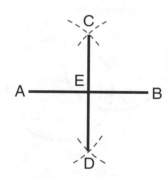

1. With A as center and a radius greater than one-half $\overline{AB}$, draw arcs above and below $\overline{AB}$.
2. With B as center and with the same radius, draw arcs intersecting the first arcs drawn. Label the points of intersection of the arcs C and D.
3. Draw a straight mark through C and D.
4. Use E to label the point where $\overleftrightarrow{CD}$ intersects $\overline{AB}$.
5. E is the midpoint of $\overline{AB}$.
6. Also, line CD is perpendicular to segment AB, therefore $\overleftrightarrow{CD}$ is the perpendicular bisector of $\overline{AB}$.

Name: _____ Date: _____

Bisect a Line Segment: Exercises

1. Measure $\overline{AE}$ and $\overline{EB}$ on the diagram in B on page 58. Are they the same length? _____

2. Select some other point K on $\overline{CD}$. Measure the distance from K to A and from K to B.

    a)   How do these distances compare? _____

    b)   Do you think that any point on $\overline{CD}$ is the same distance from A and B? _____

3. Use the corner of an index card to determine where the four angles with vertex E are right angles.

4. Construct the perpendicular bisector of each of the following line segments.

    a)   b)

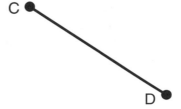

5. Below are two triangles. Carefully construct the perpendicular bisector of each side of each triangle.

    a)   b)

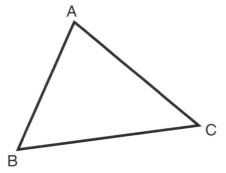

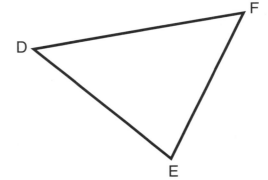

    c)   Did the perpendicular bisectors of the sides of triangle ABC meet in the same point?

          _____

    d)   Did the perpendicular bisectors of the sides of triangle DEF meet in the same point?

          _____

    e)   Try to draw a circle that passes through the three vertices of one of the triangles.

Name: _____ Date: _____

The three perpendicular bisectors of the sides of the triangle meet in the same point, that is, they are congruent. **Concurrent** lines are lines that have a point in common. In the completed diagram that follows, the perpendicular bisectors of the sides of the triangle meet at point O.

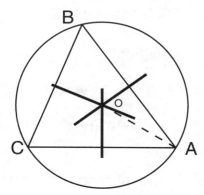

The point O is the same distance from the vertices A, B, and C. A circle with O as a center and $\overline{OA}$ as a radius will contain the points A, B, and C. The circle O is **circumscribed** about the triangle ABC. The point O is the **circumcenter** of the triangle ABC. The triangle ABC is **inscribed** in circle O because its three vertices belong to the set of points in the circle.

C.   Construct a Ray Perpendicular to a Line at a Given Point in the Line

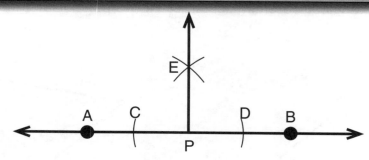

$\overleftrightarrow{AB}$ is a line with P a point in the line. A ray is to be constructed so that it is perpendicular to $\overleftrightarrow{AB}$ at P.

1. Using your compass, use P as the center and mark points C and D on $\overleftrightarrow{AB}$ so that $\overline{PC}$ ≅ $\overline{PD}$.
2. With C as center and with a radius greater than $\overline{PC}$, draw an arc in the half plane on one side of $\overleftrightarrow{AB}$.
3. With D as center and with the same radius, draw an arc that intersects the arc with center C.
4. Label E the point of intersection of the arcs.
5. Draw $\overrightarrow{PE}$.
6. $\overrightarrow{PE}$ is perpendicular to $\overleftrightarrow{AB}$.

Name: _____ Date: _____

Construct a Perpendicular Ray: Exercises

1. Use the corner of an index card to test the two angles at P in the diagram in section C on page 60 to determine whether they are right angles.

2. Below are two line segments. Construct a perpendicular at each point labeled P.

    a)

    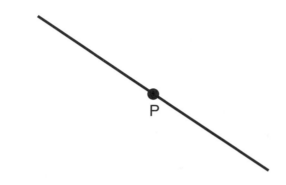

    b)

3. Construct perpendiculars to segment AB at the points A and B.

    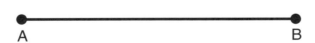

Name: _____ Date: _____

D. Construct a Perpendicular From a Point to a Line

$\overleftrightarrow{AB}$ is a line and P is a point not in $\overleftrightarrow{AB}$. Construct a perpendicular from P to $\overleftrightarrow{AB}$.

1. With P as center, draw an arc that intersects $\overleftrightarrow{AB}$ in two points.
2. Label these points C and D.
3. With C as center and with a radius greater than one-half $\overline{CD}$, draw an arc in the half plane not containing P.
4. With D as center and with the same radius, draw an arc that intersects the arc with C as center.
5. Label E the point where the two arcs intersect.
6. Draw $\overrightarrow{PE}$.
7. $\overleftrightarrow{PE}$ is perpendicular to $\overleftrightarrow{AB}$.
8. Label K the point where $\overrightarrow{PE}$ intersects $\overleftrightarrow{AB}$.

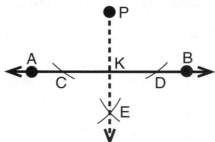

Construct Perpendicular from a Point to a Line: Exercises

1. Use the corner of an index card to test the four angles at vertex K to determine whether they are right angles.

2. $\overleftrightarrow{AB}$ and $\overleftrightarrow{CD}$ are two different lines. P is a point not in either line. From P construct a perpendicular to each of the lines.

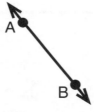
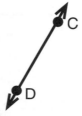

P

The distance from a given point P to a line is the length of the segment that is perpendicular to the line and that has P as one endpoint and a point in the line as the other endpoint. In the exercise above, the segments from P to $\overleftrightarrow{AB}$ and $\overleftrightarrow{CD}$ were constructed. The distance from P to each of the lines is measured along the perpendicular segment.

3. Construct a perpendicular from M to the line XY. In this case, first extend the line to the left of point X.

M

X   Y

Name: _____ Date: _____

    The length of each **altitude** of a triangle is a distance from a point to a line. For triangle ABC that follows, the three altitudes are shown. The length of segment $\overline{CD}$ is the distance from C to $\overleftrightarrow{AB}$, and $\overline{CD}$ is the altitude to base $\overleftrightarrow{AB}$ of the triangle. Likewise, $\overline{BF}$ is the altitude to base $\overline{AC}$, and $\overline{AE}$ is the altitude to base $\overleftrightarrow{BC}$. Every triangle has three altitudes. The three altitudes of a triangle are concurrent.

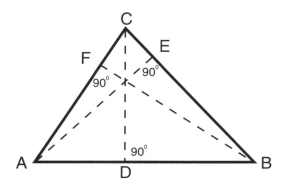

4. Carefully construct the three altitudes of each of the following triangles.

    a) This is an acute triangle. Are the three altitudes concurrent; that is, do they all meet at the same point?

        _____

        If so, was the point of concurrency inside, in, or outside the triangle?

        _____

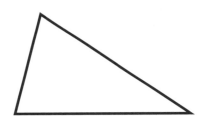

    b) This is a right triangle. Were the three altitudes concurrent?

        _____

        Did you need to construct all three altitudes?

        _____

    c) This is an obtuse triangle. Are the three altitudes concurrent?

        _____

        If so, where is the point of concurrency?

        _____

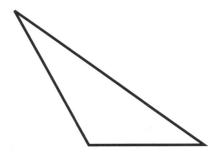

Name: _____ Date: _____

E. Bisect a Given Angle

To bisect the angle ABC means to locate a ray BF so that angle ABF is congruent to angle CBF.

1. Use B as center, and with a convenient radius, draw arcs that intersect rays BA and BC.
2. Label the points of intersection D and E.
3. With a convenient radius, and with D as center, draw an arc in the interior of angle ABC.
4. With the same radius, and with E as center, draw an arc that intersects the arc with center D.
5. Label the point of intersection F.
6. Draw ray BF.
7. Ray BF is the bisector of angle ABC.

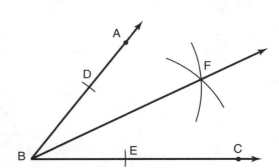

Bisect a Given Angle: Exercises

1. Construct the bisector of each of the angles below.

a)

b)

2. Below are two triangles. For each triangle, construct the three angle bisectors.

a)

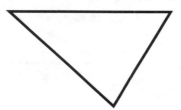

b)

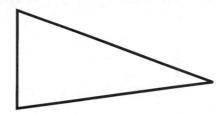

The three angle bisectors meet at a point called the **incenter** of the triangle. The point O is the same distance from each side of the triangle.

With O as center and with a radius equal to the distance from O to $\overline{AB}$, a circle may be drawn that contains one point in each side of the triangle. The circle is said to be **inscribed** in the triangle. The triangle is said to be **circumscribed** about the circle.

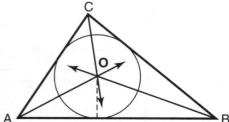

Name: _____ Date: _____

F.   Construct an Angle Congruent to a Given Angle

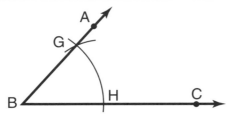 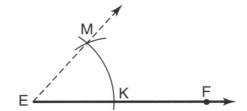

Construct an angle congruent to ∠ABC.

1.   Use some ray EF as a side of the angle to be constructed and use E for the vertex.
2.   With B as center and with some convenient radius, draw an arc that intersects the sides of angle ABC at G and H.
3.   With E as center and with the same radius, draw an arc that intersects $\overline{EF}$ at K.
4.   Using K as center and $\overline{GH}$ as radius, draw an arc that intersects at M the arc whose center is E.
5.   Draw $\overrightarrow{EM}$.
6.   Angle MEF is congruent to angle ABC.
7.   Trace angle ABC on thin paper. Then place the drawing over angle MEF to see if the two angles are the same size.

Construct Congruent Angles: Exercises

Below are two angles. Construct an angle congruent to each.

1.

2.

G. Construct a Triangle Congruent to a Given Triangle

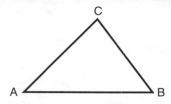 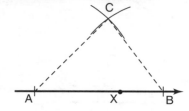

1. Draw any ray A¹X.
2. Use your compass to measure $\overline{AB}$.
3. With A¹ as one endpoint, mark a point on $\overrightarrow{A^1X}$ so that $\overline{A^1B^1} \cong \overline{AB}$.
4. With $\overline{AC}$ as a radius and A¹ as center, draw an arc above $\overline{A^1B^1}$.
5. With $\overline{BC}$ as radius and B¹ as center, draw an arc that intersects the first arc.
6. Label C¹ the point where the arcs intersect.
7. Draw $\overline{A^1C^1}$ and $\overline{B^1C^1}$.
8. Triangles ABC and A¹B¹C¹ are congruent.

Construct Congruent Triangles: Exercise

Construct a triangle congruent to the given triangle.

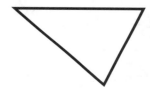

H. Construct a Line Through a Given Point and Parallel to a Given Line

Through P, construct a line parallel to $\overleftrightarrow{AB}$.

1. Through P, draw any line that intersects $\overleftrightarrow{AB}$ at some point C.
2. With P as a vertex and with $\overleftrightarrow{CP}$ as one side, construct an angle EPD congruent to angle ACP.
3. The line DP is the required line.

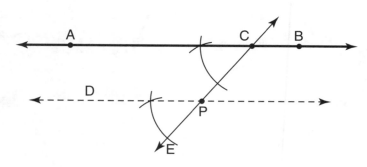

One of the assumptions in Euclidean geometry is that a given point not in a given line is in one and only one line parallel to the given line. This was Euclid's famous **Fifth Postulate**, which is historically significant.

Name: _____ Date: _____

I. Construct a Line Parallel to a Given Line and at a Given Distance From It

$\overleftrightarrow{AB}$ is the given line and **d** is the segment representing the distance between $\overleftrightarrow{AB}$ and the line parallel to $\overleftrightarrow{AB}$.

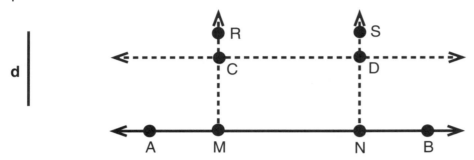

1. At two points M and N on $\overleftrightarrow{AB}$, construct perpendiculars $\overrightarrow{MR}$ and $\overrightarrow{NS}$.
2. With M as one endpoint, lay off on ray MR a segment MC congruent to **d**.
3. With N as one endpoint, lay off on ray NS a segment ND congruent to **d**.
4. Draw $\overleftrightarrow{CD}$.
5. $\overleftrightarrow{CD}$ is the required line.

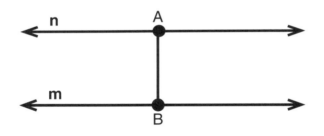

The distance between two parallel lines is the length of a segment with an endpoint in each line and perpendicular to the lines.

In the picture, **n** and **m** represent parallel lines. $\overline{AB}$ has one endpoint in **n** and one endpoint in **m**. $\overline{AB}$ is perpendicular to both lines. The length of $\overline{AB}$ is the distance between **n** and **m**.

The altitude of a parallelogram is an example of a distance between parallel lines.

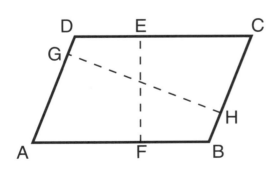

In the illustration, $\overline{EF}$ is called the altitude to either $\overline{AB}$ or $\overline{DC}$. $\overline{GH}$ is called the altitude to either $\overline{AD}$ or $\overline{BC}$.

Name: _____ Date: _____

Construct Parallel Lines: Exercise

You are an engineer responsible for designing the layout of a new city. The city will be located next to a river that runs north-northeast. The southern boundary of the city will be the highway running east to west. Main Street will be the road that runs north to south.

Your job is to map out seven city streets parallel to the highway, five city streets parallel to Main Street, and two city streets parallel to the river. Of the five city streets parallel to Main Street, three must be on the west side of Main Street and two on the east side of Main Street. The only tools you may use are a straightedge and a compass.

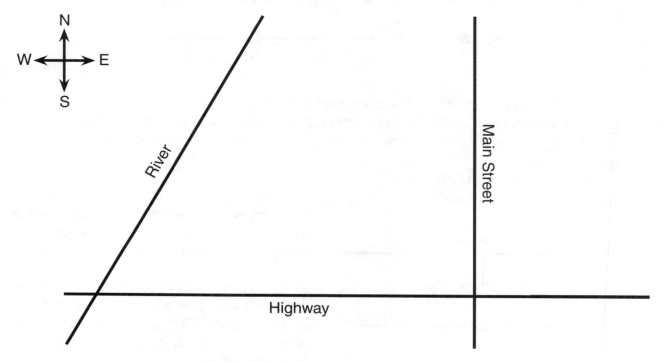

Use a protractor for the following questions.

1. What is the measure of each angle in the intersection of the river with the highway?

    _____

2. What is the measure of each angle in the intersection of Main Street with the highway?

    _____

3. Write the measure of each angle in the intersection of the two streets parallel with the river and their intersections with the highway.

    _____

4. At some point, the streets parallel to Main Street will intersect the streets parallel to the river. What are the measures of the angles at these intersections?

    _____

Name: _____   Date: _____

J. Separate a Circle Into Six Congruent Arcs

1. Draw a circle with any convenient radius.
2. Using the same radius and any point A in the circle as center, draw an arc that intersects the circle at B.
3. Using the same radius and B as center, draw an arc that intersects the circle at C.
4. Continue this procedure until you have separated the circle into six consecutive arcs.

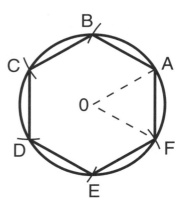

This particular construction is at the basis of many designs. Connecting consecutive points makes a regular hexagon. It is possible to bisect the arcs and to connect consecutive points to make a regular dodecagon (12-sided polygon).

The following designs are based upon this construction.

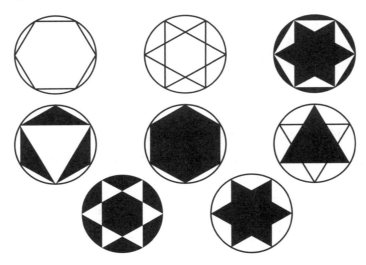

Separate a Circle Into Six Congruent Arcs: Exercise

Use this space to make a design of your own.

Name: _____ Date: _____

Constructions: Exercises

1. Using $\overline{AB}$ as one side, construct a triangle with each of the sides congruent to $\overline{AB}$. If three sides of a triangle are congruent, the triangle is a(n) _____ triangle.

A   B

2. Using $\overline{AB}$ as one side and $\overline{AC}$ as one of two congruent sides, construct a triangle ABC. If at least two sides of a triangle are congruent, the triangle is a(n) _____ triangle.

A   B

A   C

Name: _____ Date: _____

3. Using your ruler and compass, carefully construct four triangles, each with sides congruent to these given segments.

a
_____

b
_____

c
_____

Trace one triangle and place the tracing over each of the other three triangles.

a) Can you match the sides and angles? _____

b) Are the triangles the same size? _____

c) What conclusion can you draw? _____

_____

_____

Name: _____ Date: _____

4. Using your ruler and compass, carefully construct four triangles, each with two sides con-
    gruent to $\overline{AB}$ and $\overline{AC}$ and one angle congruent to angle A. The letters will tell you how the
    angle is related to the two given sides.

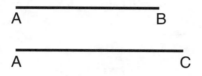

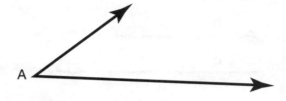

Trace one triangle and place the tracing over each of the other three triangles.

    a)   Can you match the sides and angles? _____

    b)   Are the triangles the same size? _____

    c)   What conclusion can you draw? _____

_____

_____

_____

Name: _____ Date: _____

5. Using your ruler and compass, carefully construct four triangles, each with a side congru-
    ent to $\overline{AB}$ and with two angles congruent to the angles A and B. The letters will tell you
    how the angles are related to the given side.

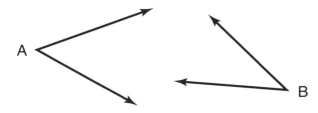

Trace one triangle and place the tracing over each of the other three triangles.

   a) Can you match the sides and angles? _____

   b) Are the triangles the same size? _____

   c) What conclusion can you draw? _____

       _____

       _____

       _____

Name: _____ Date: _____

6. Construct a square ABCD with sides congruent to the given segment AB.

$$\overline{}$$

A   B

7. Use the given line segments to construct a rectangle ABCD.

8. Use a compass to find the measure in inches of each of the segments below.

     1 inch: ————————

a)   ————————————————————————

b)   ——————————————

c)   ————————————————————————————

9. Use a compass to find the measure in centimeters of each of the segments below.

     1 centimeter: ——

a)   ————————————————————————

b)   ——————————————————

c)   ————————————————————

Name: _____ Date: _____

10. There are 10 centimeters in a decimeter. Use a compass to construct a segment that is one decimeter long.

11. Construct a segment that is four centimeters long. Then use this segment to construct an equilateral triangle with sides four centimeters long.

12. In the space below, complete the following steps.

   a)   Draw a circle with a diameter of three inches.
   b)   Draw a diameter and label the endpoints A and B.
   c)   Label some other point C on the circle.
   d)   Draw segments AC and BC.
   e)   Measure angle ACB.

   f)   What seems to be true of angle ACB? _____

Triangle ACB is a triangle **inscribed** in a semicircle, and thus angle ACB is an angle inscribed in a semicircle. An angle inscribed in a semicircle is a right angle.

Name: _____ Date: _____

13. A, B, and C are any three distinct points on one line, and D, E, and F are any three distinct points on another line.

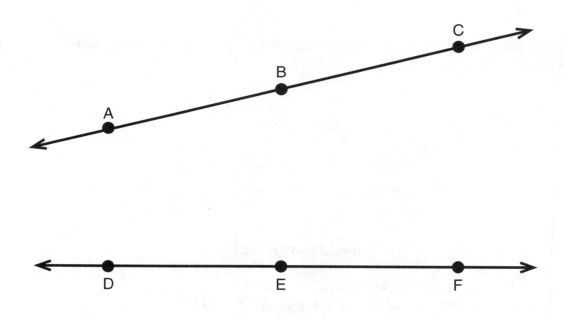

a) Draw $\overline{AE}$ and $\overline{BD}$. Label their point of intersection X.
b) Draw $\overline{AF}$ and $\overline{CD}$. Label their point of intersection Y.
c) Draw $\overline{BF}$ and $\overline{CE}$. Label their point of intersection Z.
d) Draw a line through points X and Z.

e) What did you discover about point Y? _____

_____

_____

That the points X, Y, and Z are collinear is an interesting geometrical relationship that can be easily constructed with a ruler. The proof that the three points are collinear belongs to projective geometry and not to Euclidean geometry. This relationship was discovered by one of the last great Greek mathematicians, Pappus, around A.D. 300.

Name: _____ Date: _____

Constructions: Geometric Patterns and Addition

Interesting geometric patterns may be created by using arrays arranged like the ones below. A dot is placed with each numeral, and line segments are drawn to show equal sums. The dots serve as endpoints of the segments. Notice that the arrangement of the numerals results in a one-more and one-less pattern.

Give students the idea and then let them create and color their own patterns.

1. This array can be used for the basic facts for the number 11.

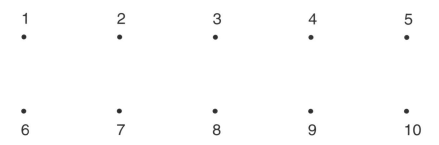

Connect 1 and 10, 2 and 9, 3 and 8, 4 and 7, and 5 and 6. Notice that $1 + 10 = 11$, $2 + 9 = 11$, $3 + 8 = 11$, $4 + 7 = 11$, and $5 + 6 = 11$. Notice that if you start with the bottom row of numerals, you illustrate the commutative principle of addition because $6 + 5 = 11$, $7 + 4 = 11$, and so on. The segments are drawn in the illustration below.

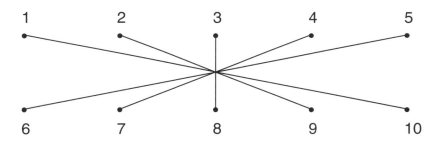

2. The same array may be used to give another pattern.

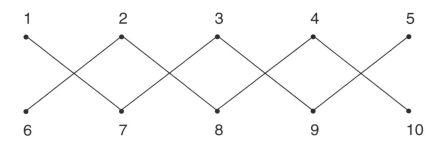

Notice that $1 + 7 = 8$ and $2 + 6 = 8$, $2 + 8 = 10$ and $3 + 7 = 10$, $3 + 9 = 12$ and $4 + 8 = 12$, and $4 + 10 = 14$ and $5 + 9 = 14$. The segments have been drawn to show these sums.

Name: _____ Date: _____

3. Finally, if all of the segments are drawn to show pairs of equal sums, the following pattern will result.

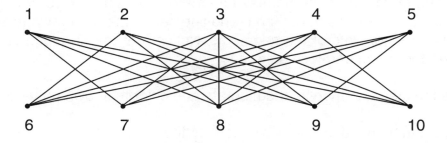

Use the space below to create your own arrays.

Constructions: Paper Folding

Paper folding can offer a wealth of ideas for helping students develop intuitive notions of geometry. Ordinary paper, waxed paper, newspaper, pages from old magazines, and so forth may be used. (Be sure you have permission to cut up newspapers or magazines.)

There are only three basic folds—one to bisect a segment, one to bisect an angle, and one to make a perpendicular from a point to a line.

1. To bisect a line segment, crease the paper sharply to make a segment as shown at right.

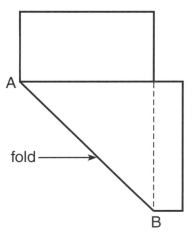

Then fold the paper over so that the ends of the segment coincide and again crease the paper sharply.

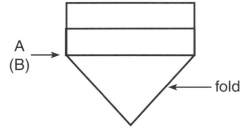

Unfold the paper. The second crease represents the perpendicular bisector of the segment.

This technique is used to find the midpoint of the side of a triangle or other polygon, to make a right angle, to construct the perpendicular bisector of the side of a triangle, and so on.

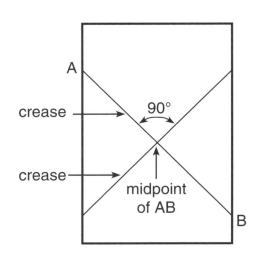

2. To bisect an angle, fold the paper so that the two sides of the angle coincide, then make a sharp crease along the fold.

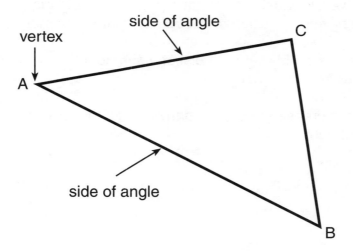

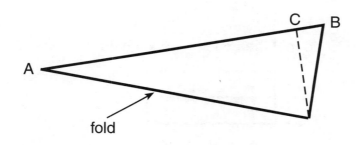

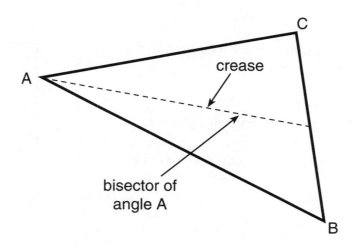

3. To fold a perpendicular from a point to a line, first crease the paper to locate a segment. Then make a dot to represent a point.

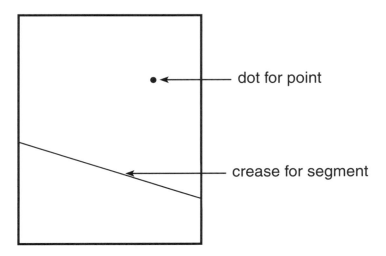

Now fold the paper so that the dot is on the fold and the parts of the line segment are over one another.

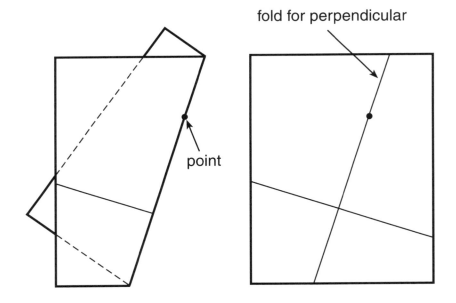

This technique may be used to fold the altitudes of a triangle.

Name: _____ Date: _____

Constructions: Paper-Folding Exercises

1. Practice folding paper to make a segment and an angle, to bisect a line segment, to make a right angle, and to bisect an angle.

2. Fold a triangle.

3. Fold a quadrilateral.

4. Fold a rectangle.

5. Fold a pentagon.

6. Cut out a triangular region. Find the midpoint of each side. Then make folds over each pair of midpoints as shown. The dotted lines are folds.

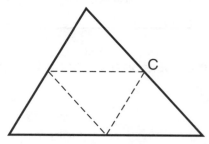

   What discoveries can you make? _____

   _____

7. Cut out a general quadrilateral region. Find the midpoint of each side. Then make folds over each pair of midpoints as shown. The dotted lines are folds.

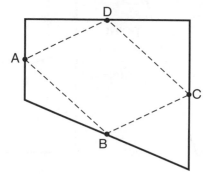

   a) What discoveries can you make? _____

   _____

   b) Compare the lengths of $\overline{AB}$ and $\overline{CD}$. _____

   c) Compare the lengths of $\overline{AD}$ and $\overline{BC}$. _____

   d) What seems to be true of ABCD? _____

Name: _____ Date: _____

8. Cut out four different triangles to use in the exercises that follow.

    a) Bisect each angle of a triangle by folding. What seems to be true of the three angle bisectors?

    _____

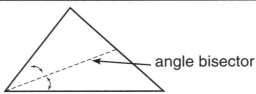

    b) By folding, locate the perpendicular bisector of each side of a triangle. What seems to be true of the three perpendicular bisectors?

    _____

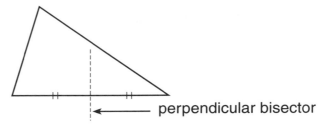

    c) By folding, locate the three altitudes of a triangle. What seems to be true of the three altitudes?

    _____

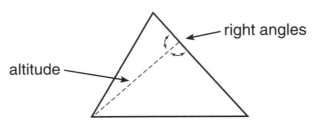

    d) By folding, locate the three medians. A **median** of a triangle is the segment with a vertex and the midpoint of the opposite side as endpoints.

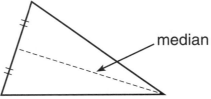

        The three medians should meet in a point, which is the **centroid** (center of gravity) of the triangular region. Use the triangle you have just made as a pattern. Cut out a triangular region from heavy, uniform cardboard. Mark a point to show the centroid you found. See whether this triangular region will balance on a pinpoint placed at the centroid.

Space Figures

Space figures are sets of points that are not all in the same plane. Just as there are closed curves in a plane, there are closed surfaces in spaces. Among the common space figures introduced in middle-school mathematics are cones, spheres, pyramids, prisms, and cylinders.

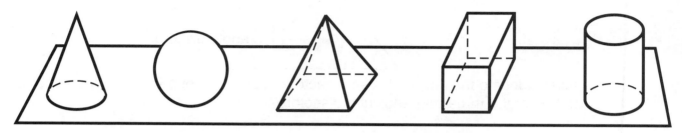

Each of these space figures consists only of the set of points on the surface. For example, a basketball is a good model of a sphere, an empty chalk box is a good model of a rectangular prism, and an empty coffee can is a good model of a cylinder.

A simple closed surface is a set of points in space that separates space into three sets of points: the set of points **in** the simple closed space figure, the set of points **in the interior** of the figure, and the set of points **in the exterior** of the figure.

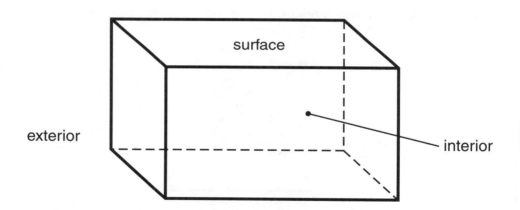

The set of points in a simple closed plane curve in union with the set of points in the interior of the curve is a **plane region**. A sheet of paper is a model of a plane region. Likewise, in space geometry, the set of points in a simple closed surface in union with the set of points in the interior of the surface is a **space region**. A tennis ball is a model of a simple closed surface, known as a sphere, while an orange is a model of a spherical region.

In **plane geometry**, we work with two dimensions: length and width. In **solid geometry**, we work with three dimensions: length, width, and height. Although the surface of a sheet of paper has only two dimensions, we can picture three-dimensional figures. For prisms and pyramids, the edges we can see are represented by solid marks, and the edges we cannot see are represented by dashed marks. For example, here are pictures of a rectangular prism and a triangular pyramid.

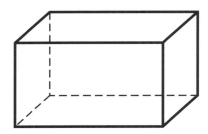 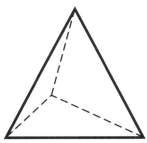

In order to describe prisms and pyramids, three special words are needed. The **faces** are the flat sides of the prism. A rectangular prism has six rectangular regions as faces.

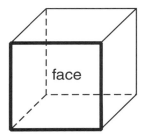

The **edges** are line segments, each of which is the intersection of two faces. A rectangular prism has 12 edges.

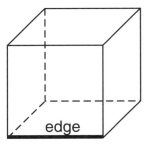

The **vertices** (plural of vertex) are points of intersection of three edges. A rectangular prism has eight vertices.

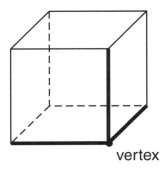

Name: _____ Date: _____

Prisms

Fold a sheet of paper lengthwise as shown in the illustration below.

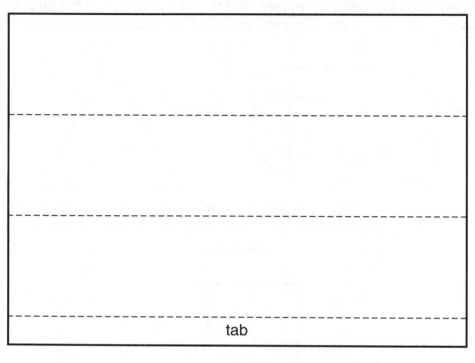

tab

Next, make the sheet into a triangular tube, which is open at both ends, and secure the tab with transparent tape.

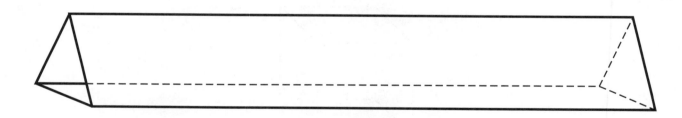

1. What is the shape of each side? _____

2. What is the shape of each end? _____

3. Stand the tube on end on a horizontal surface. Is it perpendicular to the surface?

   _____

4. Do the two triangular ends lie in parallel planes? _____

Prisms with bases other than triangles can be created in this same way by making more folds in the paper.

Imagine that the two triangular ends are regions and that the resulting figure now has five sides; that is, two triangular regions as ends and three rectangular regions as sides. This sealed, **empty** tube represents a space figure known as a **triangular prism**; specifically a right triangular prism, since the sides are perpendicular to the bases.

Only **right prisms** are to be considered in this unit. The lateral faces are rectangular regions and are perpendicular to the bases. In children's language, "They stand straight up and down."

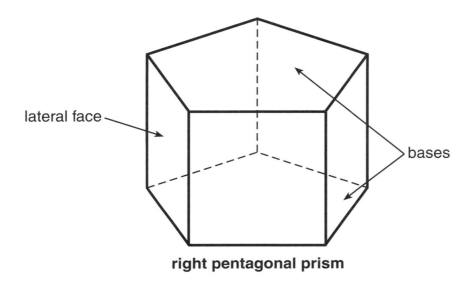

right pentagonal prism

Other prisms are shaped so that the lateral faces are not perpendicular to the bases. In children's language, "They lean to one side."

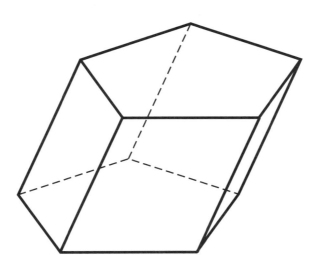

prism that is not a right prism

Name: _____ Date: _____

Patterns for Prisms

1. This is a pattern for a triangular prism.

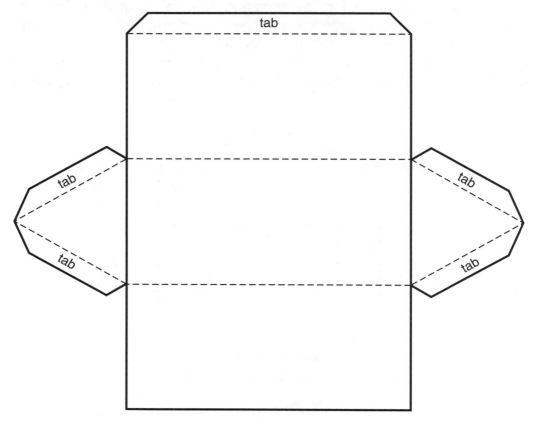

You may make models of this prism by tracing the pattern or making copies of this page. Cut the pattern out along the solid marks, and fold along the dashed marks. Tape or glue the tabs to the rectangular sides of the prism.

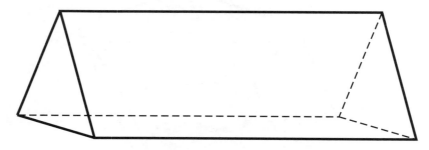

a) A triangular prism has _____ triangular faces and _____ rectangular faces.

b) A triangular prism has _____ vertices.

c) A triangular prism has _____ edges.

Name: _____ Date: _____

2. This is a pattern for a rectangular prism.

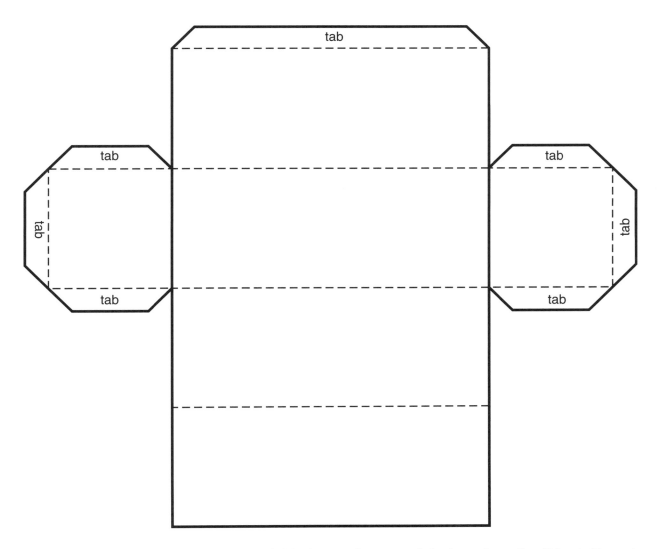

When the pattern is cut out and folded to make a model of a prism, it will look like a box.

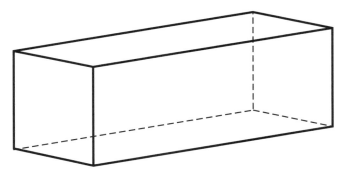

a) A rectangular prism has _____ rectangular faces, _____ edges, and _____ vertices.

Name: _____ Date: _____

3. This is a pattern for a pentagonal prism.

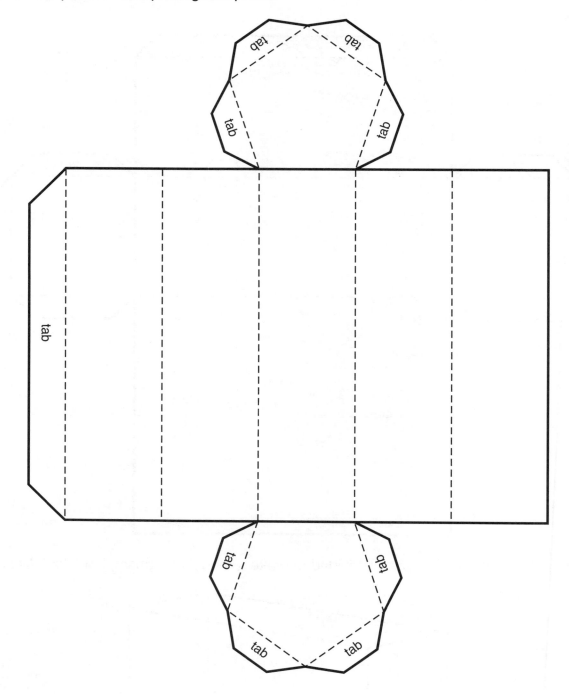

a) A pentagonal prism has _____ pentagonal faces and _____ rectangular faces,

making _____ faces in all.

b) It has _____ vertices and _____ edges.

Name: _____ Date: _____

4. The following table names and describes four kinds of right prisms. Complete the table under the bases and number of vertices, edges, and faces. Can you discover any pattern?

Kind of Right Prism	Parallel Bases	Number of Vertices	Number of Edges	Number of Faces
a) Triangular Prism 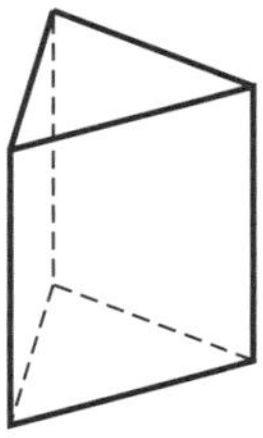	Triangular Regions	6	9	5
b) Quadrilateral Prism 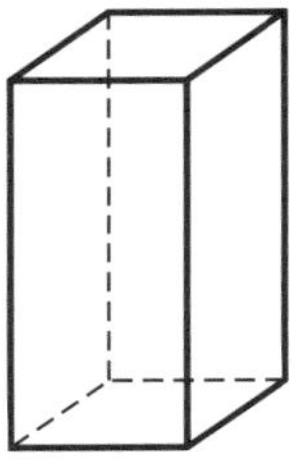				
c) Pentagonal Prism 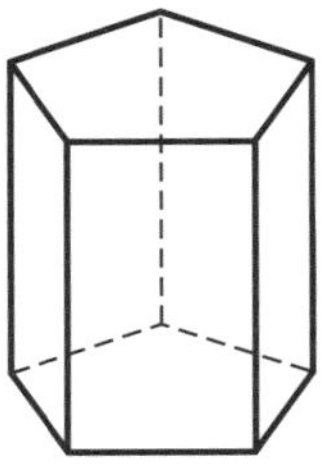				
d) Hexagonal Prism 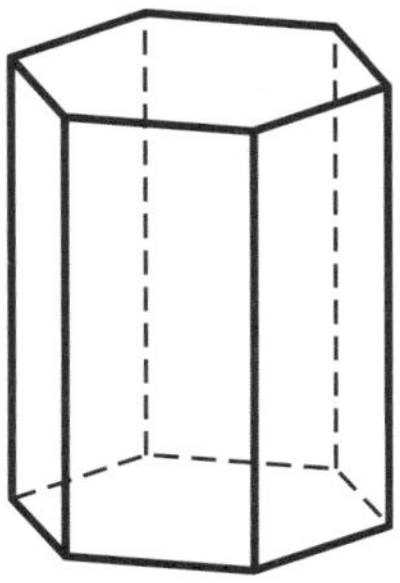				

Patterns for Pyramids

Another kind of space figure is the pyramid. Trace or make copies of the following patterns and use them to make models of pyramids.

1. This is a pattern for a triangular pyramid or tetrahedron.

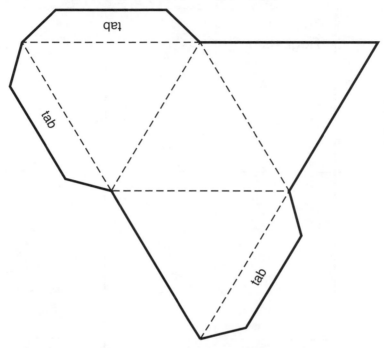

2. This is a pattern for a quadrilateral (or quadrangular) pyramid.

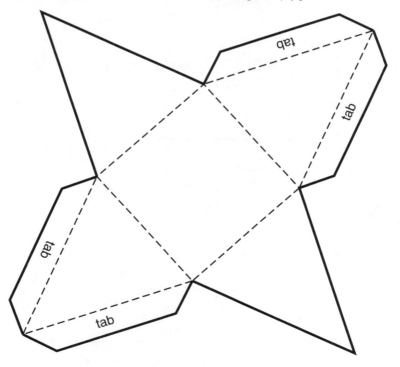

Name: _____ Date: _____

3. This is a pattern for a pentagonal pyramid.

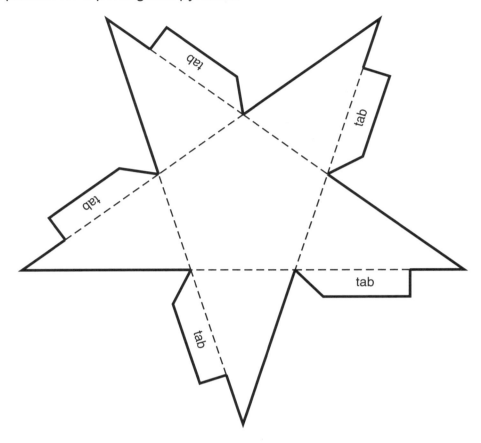

Pyramids are classified according to the shape of the polygonal region forming the base. For example, the following is a quadrilateral pyramid.

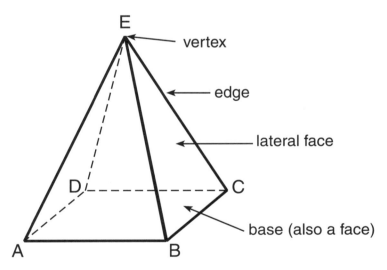

4. For a pyramid, the lateral faces are triangular regions. The above pyramid has _____ faces, _____ vertices, and _____ edges.

Name: _____ Date: _____

5. The following table names and describes four kinds of pyramids. Complete the table under the bases and number of vertices, edges, and faces. Can you discover any pattern?

Kind of Pyramid	Base	Number of Vertices	Number of Edges	Number of Faces
a) Triangular Pyramid	Triangular Region	4	6	4
b) Quadrilateral Pyramid				
c) Pentagonal Pyramid				
d) Hexagonal Pyramid				

Cylinders

The most familiar type of cylinder, and the one usually considered in middle-school mathematics, is the **right circular cylinder**. The two bases of the cylinder are congruent circular regions that lie in parallel planes. A segment with the two centers as endpoints is perpendicular to both bases. Also, segments with corresponding points in the boundaries of each circular region are perpendicular to both bases.

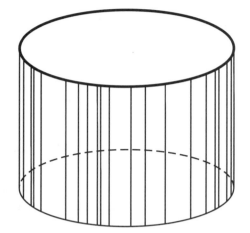

Examine an ordinary tin can. Think about what the parts of the can must have looked like before they were put together. If you are not sure, get a can opener and cut a can apart. Actually, you can tell what the curved (lateral) surface would look like by making a perpendicular cut in the label on the can, peeling it off the can, and flattening it out. The can now consists of a rectangular region and two congruent circular regions.

A right circular cylinder is only one kind of cylinder. The following diagrams illustrate some other cylinders.

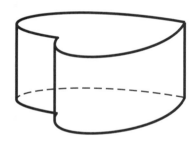 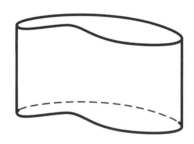 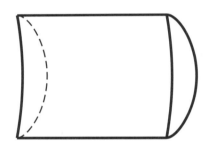

The bases, which are simple closed regions at the ends of the cylinders, are congruent and parallel. The surface or surfaces that join the boundaries of the bases are called the lateral faces.

Cylinders can have bases other than circular regions. The following are examples of shapes that the bases of a cylinder may have.

A right circular cylinder is the only one usually considered in middle-school mathematics. However, students may be made aware of other models of cylinders commonly found around the home. An ordinary sardine can, a plastic toothbrush container with oval ends, a rounded clothes hamper designed to fit into a square corner, and so on, are types of cylinders.

This is a pattern for a right circular cylinder.

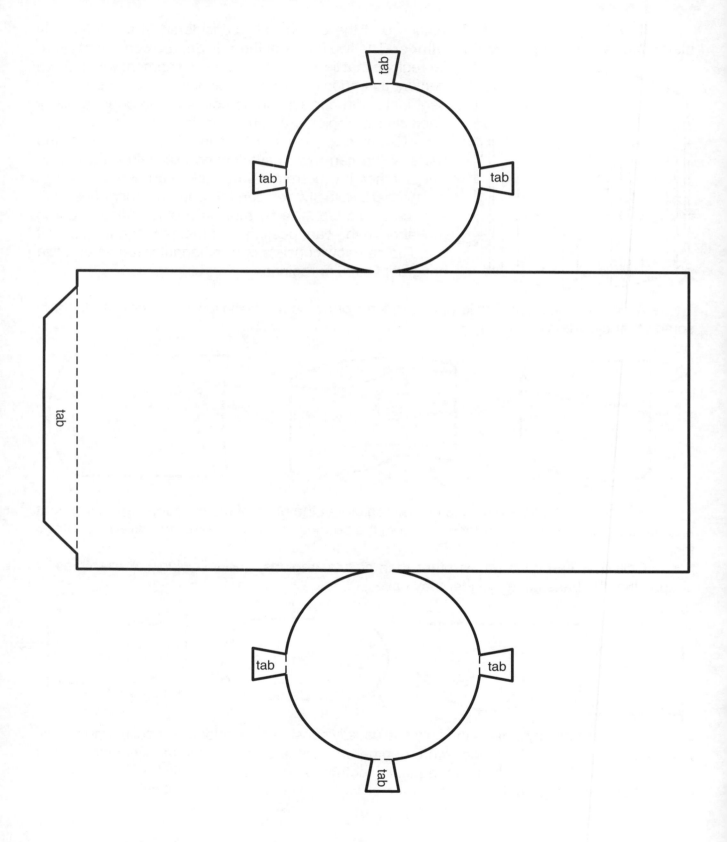

Name: _____ Date: _____

Spheres

The geometric shape suggested by the surface of a ball is a **sphere**. A sphere, like the other space figures considered in this unit, is a closed surface. In children's language, "It is a hollow ball."

Spheres: Exercises

1. If you slice straight through a hollow ball, what will be the shape of

    the rim of the cut? _____

2. Since a round orange is easier to manage than a hollow ball, use an orange for some

    experimentation.

    a) Slice the top off an orange. What is the shape of the rim of both pieces?

    _____

    b) Imagine that the orange is perfectly round. Every time you make a cut through the

        whole orange, what is the shape of the rim of the cut? _____

    c) Now slice through the orange so that you have the longest possible rim on the cut

        surfaces. What is the shape of the rim? _____

    d) In how many different ways can you slice through a whole orange so that you will

        have the longest rim on the cut surfaces? _____

    e) In how many ways can you cut the orange in half? _____

    f) How could you locate the center of the orange? _____

The above exercises were intended to help develop some intuitive notions of the intersections of planes and a sphere. If a sphere is cut by a plane, the intersection is a circle.

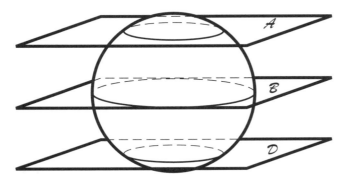

If a plane contains the center of the sphere, the intersection is a **great circle**. In the illustration, the intersection of plane *B* and the sphere is a great circle.

If a plane does not contain the center of the sphere, the intersection is a **small circle**. In the illustration, the intersection of plane *A* and the sphere is a small circle. Likewise, the intersection of plane *D* and the sphere is a small circle.

In plane geometry, the shortest distance between two points in a plane is the length of the segment with the given points as endpoints. On a sphere, the shortest distance between two points is the length of the shorter arc of the great circle that contains these two points. Airplanes take the shortest distance between cities of the earth by flying on **great circle routes**.

To locate positions on the earth's surface, a grid is formed by drawing two sets of circles.

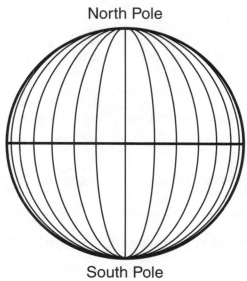

A set of great circles called **meridians** or **lines of longitude** are drawn through the North and South Poles. The **equator** is a great circle whose plane is perpendicular to the diameter with the North and South Poles as endpoints. A set of small circles called **parallels of latitude** are drawn with their planes parallel to the plane of the equator.

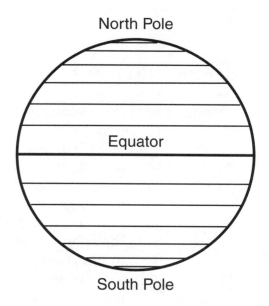

These two sets of circles form a grid. A location may be determined by the intersection of a parallel of latitude and a meridian of longitude.

North Pole

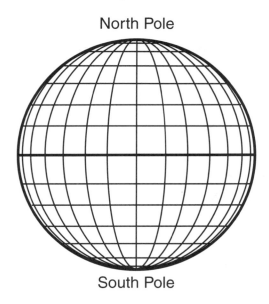

South Pole

A sphere is a closed surface, all points of which are the same distance from an interior point called the **center**. A **radius** is a segment from the center to a point on the sphere. A **diameter** is a segment that contains the center and two points of the sphere as endpoints.

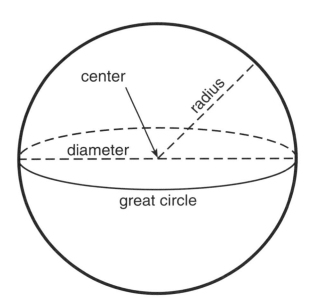

All radii of the same sphere are congruent. Also, all diameters of the same sphere are congruent.

Volumes and Surface Areas for Specific Figures

Recall all of the figures introduced thus far.

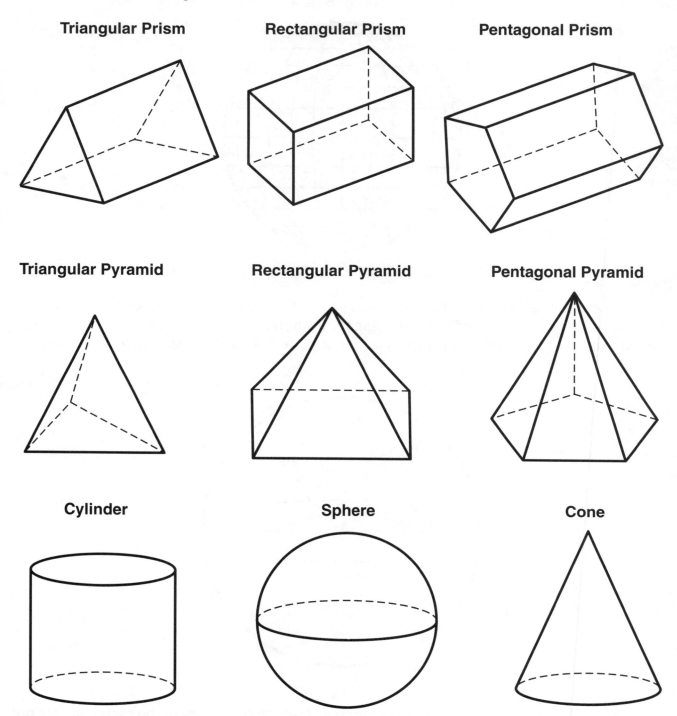

Triangular Prism   **Rectangular Prism**   **Pentagonal Prism**

Triangular Pyramid   **Rectangular Pyramid**   **Pentagonal Pyramid**

Cylinder   **Sphere**   **Cone**

Notice how the figures were grouped? All prisms were together, then all pyramids, followed by all circular figures. This grouping allows for ease in determining volumes and surface areas.

Volume and Surface Area: Prisms

Recall that lateral faces were the parallelogram-shaped faces on the sides of the prism, and the bases were the polygonal faces on the ends. To determine volumes and surface areas of any prism, all we need to know is how to find the areas of the bases, the height (or length) of the prism, and the perimeter of the base. Let's look at a rectangular prism.

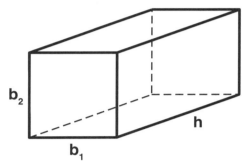

The area of the bases is just the length of the base times the height of the base as seen here.

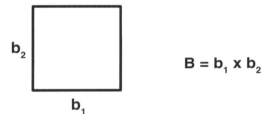

$$B = b_1 \times b_2$$

The height or length of the prism is the distance from one base to the other base. Usually the height is given by the letter **h** as seen here.

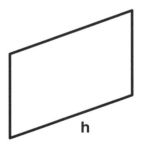

The perimeter of the base is just the distance around the base or the sum of the lengths of the sides of the base as seen here.

$$p = b_1 + b_2 + b_1 + b_2$$

Therefore, the volume of a prism is: **V = Bh**, where **B** is the area of the base figure and **h** is the height of the prism.

The surface area of a prism is **SA = LA + 2B**. **LA** is the lateral area. The **lateral area** is determined by multiplying the perimeter of the base figure times the height of the prism. **B** is the area of the base figure. This means that the surface area of a prism can be written as: **SA = ph + 2B**.

Volume and Surface Area: Pyramids

Recall that lateral faces were the triangular-shaped sides of the pyramid and the base was the polygonal face on the end. To determine volumes and surface areas of any pyramid, all we need to know is how to find the area of the base, the altitude or height of the pyramid, the slant height of the lateral faces, and the perimeter of the base. Let's look at a rectangular pyramid.

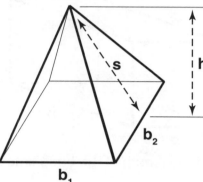

The area of the base is just the length of the base times the height of the base as seen here.

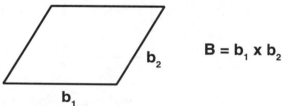

$$B = b_1 \times b_2$$

The altitude or height of the pyramid is the distance from the base to the vertex of the pyramid as seen here.

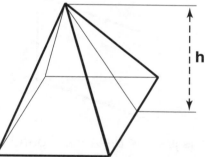

The slant height is the height of the lateral face of the pyramid, denoted by the letter **s**, as seen here.

The perimeter of the base is just the distance around the base or just the sum of the lengths of the sides of the base as seen here.

p = b$_1$ + b$_2$ + b$_1$ + b$_2$

Therefore, the volume of a pyramid is:

V = $\frac{1}{3}$Bh

where **B** is the area of the base figure and **h** is the altitude or height of the pyramid.

The surface area of a pyramid is:

SA = LA + B

LA is the lateral area. The lateral area is determined by multiplying one-half times the perimeter of the base figure times the slant height of the pyramid. **B** is the area of the base figure. This means that the surface area of a pyramid can be written as:

SA = $\frac{1}{2}$ps + B

Volume and Surface Area: Cylinders

Recall that the lateral face of a cylinder was rectangular shaped and the bases were the circular faces on the ends. To determine volumes and surface areas of any cylinder, all we need to know is how to find the areas of the bases and the height of the cylinder. Let's look at a cylinder.

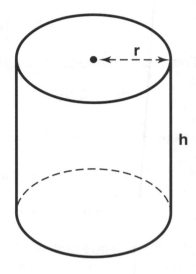

The area of the base is just the area of a circle as seen here.

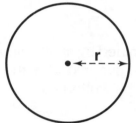

$B = \pi r^2$

The height of the cylinder is the distance from one base to the other base of the cylinder as seen here.

Therefore, the volume of a cylinder is:

V = Bh

were **B** is the area of the base figure and **h** is the height of the cylinder. The area of a circle is pi (π) times the square of the radius (**r**) of the circle. This means that the volume of the cylinder can be written as:

V = πr²h

The surface area of a cylinder is: **SA = LA + 2B**.

LA is the lateral area. The lateral area is determined by multiplying the circumference of the circular base times the height of the cylinder. **B** is the area of the base figure. This means that the surface area of a cylinder can be written as:

SA = 2πrh + 2πr²

Volume and Surface Area: Cones

A **cone** has a circular base that narrows and ends with a vertex at the top as shown below.

The cone is almost identical to the cylinder except that its volume is exactly one third the volume of a cylinder and the surface area is one-half the surface area of a cylinder. Therefore, the volume of a cone is:

$$V = \tfrac{1}{3}\pi r^2 h$$

and the surface area is:

$$SA = \pi rs + \pi r^2$$

where **s** is the slant height of the cone.

Volume and Surface Area: Spheres

Spheres differ from prisms, pyramids, cylinders, and cones in that spheres do not have base figures. Instead, the only dimension of a sphere that is needed is the radius of the sphere as shown below.

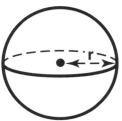

The volume of a sphere is four-thirds times pi (π) times the cube of the radius of the sphere:

$$V = \tfrac{4}{3}\pi r^3$$

The surface area of a sphere is four times pi (π) times the square of the radius of the sphere:

$$SA = 4\pi r^2$$

Name: _____ Date: _____

Volumes and Surface Areas: Exercises

1. Find the volume and surface area of a triangular prism and a triangular pyramid with the following dimensions. To find the area of the base triangle, use the following formula: **area = $\frac{1}{2}$ x length of base x height of triangle**.

    Base height is 6 cm, base length is 8 cm, the base hypotenuse is 10 cm, the height of the prism or pyramid is 12 cm, and the slant height of the pyramid is 14 cm.

2. Find the volume and surface area of a cylinder and cone with the following dimensions.

    Base radius is 4 inches, the height of the cylinder or cone is 18 inches, and the slant height of the cone is 22 inches.

Name: _____   Date: _____

3.   Find the volume and surface area of a sphere with a radius of 25 feet.

4.   Draw a regular pentagon with side lengths of 2 inches. Determine the area of this penta-
     gon. Use the formula: **area = 1.720 x a²**, in which **a** is the length of one of the sides.

     Now find the volume and surface area of a pentagonal prism and pyramid with this base,
     a height of 6 inches for the prism or pyramid, and a slant height of 8 inches for the pyra-
     mid.

Space Figures: The Five Regular Polyhedrons

A **polyhedron** is a closed space figure whose faces are portions of planes. Prisms and pyramids are polyhedrons. A polyhedron whose faces are all regular polygons and whose vertices are all alike is a **regular polyhedron**. There are only five different regular polyhedrons.

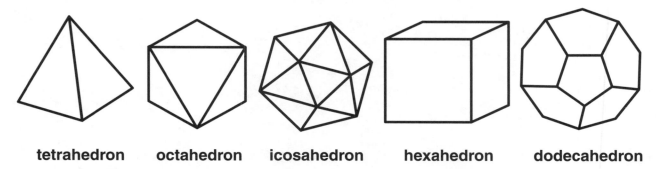

| tetrahedron | octahedron | icosahedron | hexahedron | dodecahedron |

- A **tetrahedron** (te-tre′-hē-dren) has four faces, which are equilateral triangles.

- An **octahedron** (ŏk-te′-hē-dren) has eight faces, which are equilateral triangles.

- An **icosahedron** (ī-kō-se′-hē-dren) has 20 faces, which are equilateral triangles.

- A **hexahedron** (hek-se-hē-dren), also called a cube, has six faces, which are squares.

- A **dodecahedron** (dō-dek-e′-hē-dren) has 12 faces, which are regular pentagons. This is the regular polyhedron that is often used to make novelty calendars, since there is one face for each month of the year.

The five regular polyhedrons were known to ancient mathematicians. Since all five solids were described by Plato, they are often called Platonic solids. However, they were known even before Plato's time.

The tetrahedron, cube, and octahedron are found as crystals in nature. Although the dodecahedron and icosahedron do not occur in crystal form, they have been observed as skeletons of *Radiolaria*, which are microscopic sea animals. According to Howard Eves, "In 1885, a toy regular dodecahedron of Etruscan origin was unearthed on Monet Loffa, near Padua, and is held to date back to 500 B.C."*

Patterns for these regular polyhedrons are given on the next five pages. Each figure may also be made from D-Stix, or the pattern may be run off on a colored transparency and then cut out and assembled.

*Eves, Howard. *An Introduction to the History of Mathematics,* 6th Edition. Pacific Grove, CA: Brooks/Cole, 1990. p. 92.

Tetrahedron

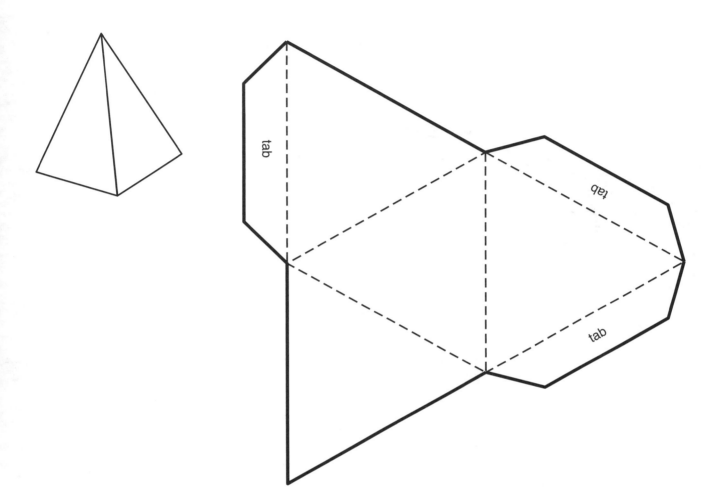

Octahedron

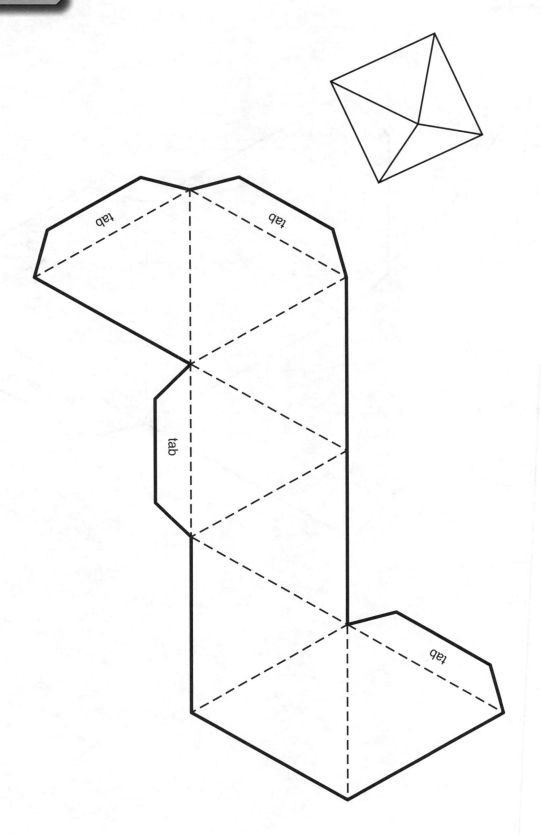

Icosahedron

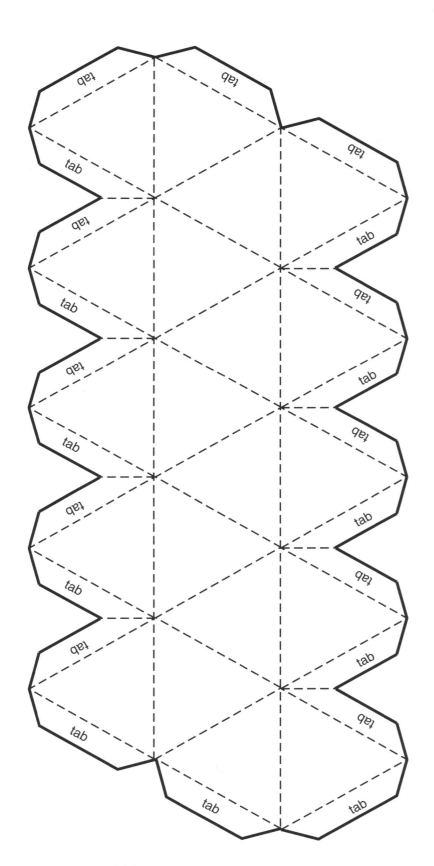

Hexahedron (Cube)

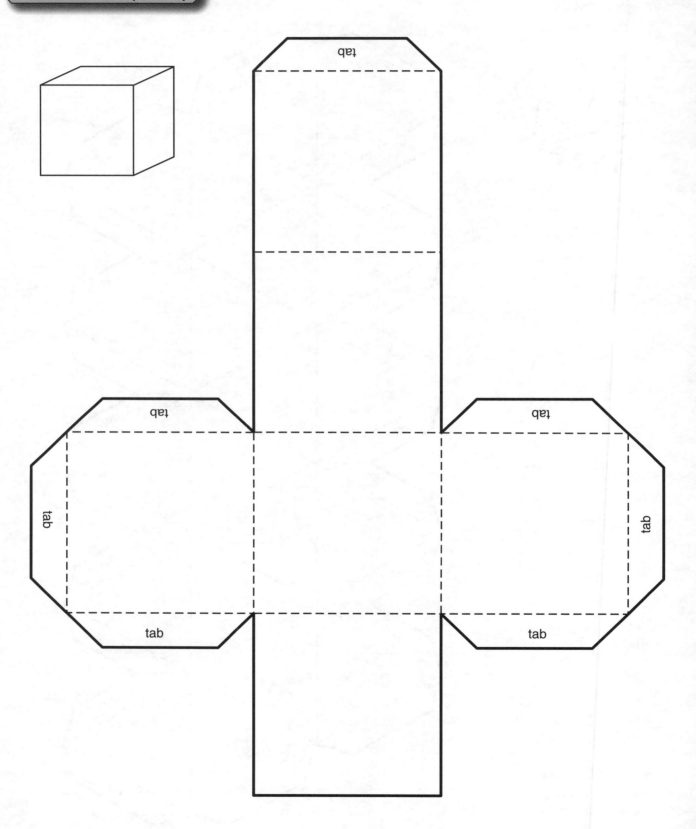

Dodecahedron

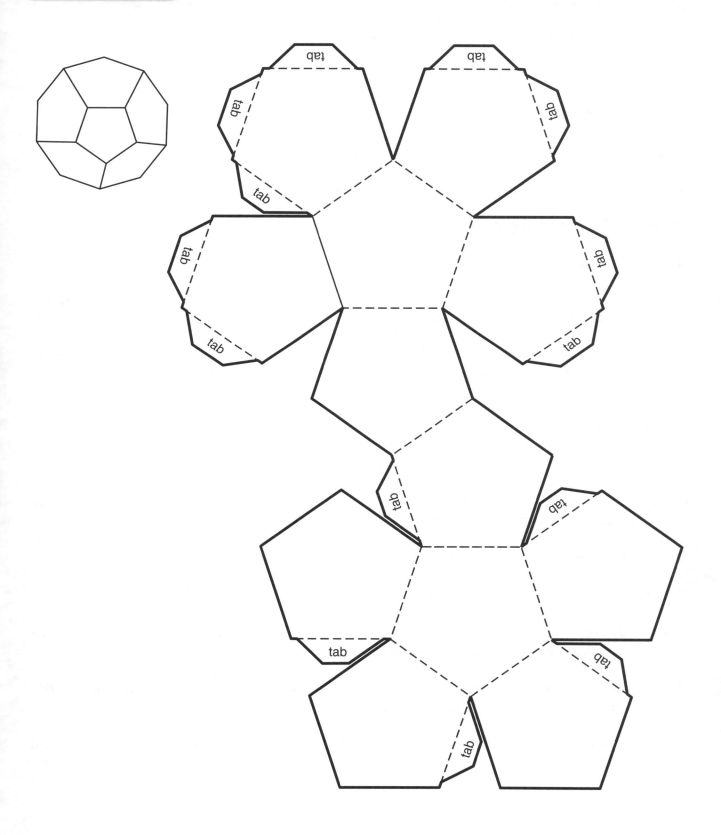

Glossary

Copies of the glossary may be made and given to students to keep in their geometry or math folders or binders. Students can then use the glossary as a quick reference tool.

Acute angle: An angle whose measure in degrees is less than 90

Acute triangle: Has all acute angles (less than 90°)

Angle: The set of points in the union of two rays with a common endpoint

Arc: A subset of the set of points in a circle

Centroid: The center of gravity of a triangular region

Chord: A line segment whose endpoints are points on the circle

Circle: A closed plane curve with each point in the curve at the same distance from a given interior point called the center

Circumscribe: To draw a plane figure around another plane figure either to intersect each vertex of the inner figure or to have each side of the outer figure tangent to the inner figure

Collinear points: Three points located so that one is between the other two

Complementary angles: Two angles whose sum is exactly 90°

Concave figure: A figure in which a line segment with endpoints in a simple closed figure contains points in the exterior of the figure

Concurrent lines: Lines that have a point in common

Congruent: When two geometric figures are exactly the same size and shape

Construction: A geometric drawing in which points and lines were determined by using only two instruments, a straightedge and a compass

Convex figure: A figure in which a line segment with endpoints in a simple closed figure contains no points in the exterior of the figure

Coplanar lines: Two lines in the same plane; any two coplanar lines either intersect or are parallel

Glossary (cont.)

Diameter: A chord (line segment) whose endpoints are collinear with the center of a circle; the center is between the endpoints of the diameter

Dodecahedron: A polyhedron with 12 faces, which are regular pentagons

Edge: A line segment that is the intersection of two faces of a space figure

Equal: Two sets that contain exactly the same elements, or two numerals that are names for the same number

Equator: A great circle on the earth whose plane is perpendicular to the diameter with the North and South Poles as endpoints

Equiangular triangle: All of its angles have the same measure

Equilateral triangle: Has three congruent sides

Euclid's Fifth Postulate: A given point not in a given line is in one and only one line parallel to the given line

Exterior: Outside a figure

Face: The flat side of a space figure

Great circle: In a plane that contains the center of a sphere, the intersection is a great circle

Hexahedron: A polyhedron with six faces, which are squares; also called a cube

Icosahedron: A polyhedron with 20 faces, which are equilateral triangles

Inscribe: To draw a plane figure inside another plane figure so that their boundaries touch at as many points as possible

Interior: Inside a figure

Intersection: Where two lines or planes meet

Isosceles triangle: Has at least two congruent sides

Line symmetry: When a line through a plane figure is such that it separates the figure so that the part on one side is an exact reflection of the part on the other side

Glossary (cont.)

Major arc: An arc identified by its endpoints and a point between the endpoints

Meridian: A great circle of the earth passing through the geographical poles and any given point on the earth's surface

Minor arc: An arc identified only by its endpoints

Noncollinear points: Three points not in a straight line

Obtuse angle: An angle whose measure in degrees is greater than 90 but less than 180

Obtuse triangle: Has one obtuse angle (greater than 90°)

Octahedron: A polyhedron with eight faces, which are equilateral triangles

Parallel lines: Coplanar lines that do not intersect

Parallelogram: A quadrilateral with its opposite sides parallel

Parallels of latitude: A set of small circles drawn with their planes parallel to the plane of the equator on earth

Pentagon: A polygon that is the union of the sets of points in five line segments

Plane geometry: Studies two dimensions: length and width

Polygon: The union of the sets of points in three or more line segments

Polygonal region: The union of the set of points in a polygon and the set of points in the interior of the polygon

Polyhedron: A closed space figure whose faces are portions of planes

Prism: A solid figure whose ends are parallel, polygonal, and congruent in size and shape and whose sides are parallelograms

Quadrilateral: A polygon that is the union of the sets of points in four line segments

Radius: The distance from the center to a point on the circle; it also may refer to the segment joining the center with a point on the circle

Ray: The union of a point and all the points in the half line to the left or right of the point; a ray has only one endpoint

Glossary (cont.)

Rectangle: A parallelogram with right angles

Regular polygon: A polygon with all of its sides congruent and all of its angles congruent

Regular polyhedron: A polyhedron whose faces are all regular polygons and whose vertices are all alike; the five regular polyhedrons are the tetrahedron, hexahedron, octahedron, dodecahedron, and icosahedron

Regular quadrilateral: A square

Regular triangle: An equilateral triangle

Rhombus: A parallelogram with adjacent sides congruent

Right angle: An angle whose measure in degrees is 90

Right circular cylinder: A cylinder whose bases are congruent circular regions that lie in parallel planes

Right prism: A prism with lateral faces that are rectangular regions and are perpendicular to the bases

Right triangle: Has one right angle (equal to 90°)

Scalene triangle: Has no congruent sides

Skew lines: Two lines that are not coplanar; they do not intersect and are not parallel

Small circle: In a plane that does not contain the center of a sphere, the intersection is a small circle

Solid geometry: Studies three dimensions: length, width, and height

Space figures: Sets of points that are not all in the same plane.

Space region: The set of points in a simple closed surface in union with the set of points in the interior of the surface

Sphere: A round solid figure having the surface equally distant from the center at all points

Square: A rectangle with adjacent sides congruent; it is also a parallelogram and a quadrilateral

Glossary (cont.)

Supplementary angles: Two angles whose sum is 180°

Surface area: The area or extent of the faces of a solid figure

Tetrahedron: A polyhedron with four faces, which are equilateral triangles

Trapezoid: A quadrilateral with one and only one pair of parallel sides

Triangle: The union of the sets of points in three line segments; it is the simplest polygon

Vertex (angles): The point of intersection of the two sides of an angle

Vertex (space figures): The point of intersection of three edges

Volume: The amount of space occupied in three dimensions

Answer Keys

Points, Lines, and Planes
Line Segment (p. 2)
You can only make one straight line to connect the two points.

Points, Lines, and Planes: Exercises (p 15–16)
Drawings will vary. Examples are given.

1.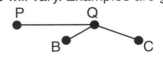

2.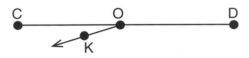

3.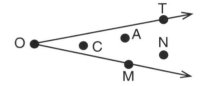

4.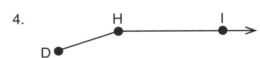

5a. $\overleftrightarrow{RA}$, $\overleftrightarrow{RY}$, $\overleftrightarrow{AY}$
b. $\overline{RA}$, $\overline{RY}$, $\overline{AY}$
c. $\overrightarrow{RA}$, $\overrightarrow{RY}$, $\overrightarrow{AY}$, $\overrightarrow{YA}$, $\overrightarrow{AR}$, $\overrightarrow{YR}$ (any three)

6.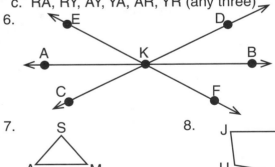

7. S, A, M 8. J, Y, U, D

9. 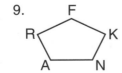 10.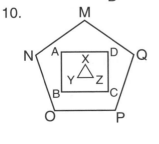

11. a. O   b. ∠AOD
c. $\overleftrightarrow{AB}$ d. $\overline{AB}$
e. ∠AOC

12. { }

Discovery Exercise (p. 17–18)
1. Teacher check.
2.

Plane	# of Points	# of Segments
A	2	1
B	3	3
C	4	6
D	5	10
E	6	15
F	7	21
	8	28
	9	36
	10	45

3. Teacher check. Accept a formula that conveys s = the sum of the number of points plus the number of segments of the plane preceding the current plane. For example, for E, add the points and segments for D. 5 + 10 = 15.

Congruence Pre-Test Activities (p. 19–22)
1. a. j   2. a. j
b. l   b. l
c. k   c. k
d. g   d. h
e. h   e. i
f. i   f. g

3. $\overline{CD}$, $\overline{EF}$ 4. ∠XYZ, ∠RST

5. a. = l.   b. = m.   c. = g.   d. = k.
e. = j.   f. = n.   i. = p.   h. = o.

Congruence: Exercises (p. 29–34)
1. a. a circle
b. Teacher check.
c. All the points were the same distance from A.
2. Repeated congruent line segments are added together to get the desired length.
a. 10 cm   b. 3 in.
3. Repeated congruent squares are added together.
a. 12 square cm
4. a. Yes   b. Yes   c. No
d. Yes   e. Yes   f. No
g. No   h. Yes   i. Yes

j. No   k. No   l. Yes
m. Yes

5.

6. No. The three angles must add up to 180°. If you use a right angle, the remaining two angles must each be less than 90°.
7. An equilateral triangle is also an isosceles triangle.
8. It is also equiangular.
9. A square is always a rhombus, but a rhombus is not always a square.
10. A rectangle is always a parallelogram, but a parallelogram is not always a rectangle.
11. A trapezoid has only one pair of parallel sides, while a parallelogram has both pairs of sides parallel.
12. No. A quadrilateral will have no parallel sides, one pair of parallel sides, or two pairs of parallel sides, so it cannot be both a trapezoid and a parallelogram at the same time.
13. a. $\angle Y$ $\angle Z$ $\angle X$
        $\overline{YZ}$ $\overline{ZX}$ $\overline{XY}$
        $\triangle YZX$

    b. $\angle C \leftrightarrow \angle E$ $\angle D \leftrightarrow \angle H$ $\angle A \leftrightarrow \angle G$
        $\angle B \leftrightarrow \angle F$
        $\overline{CD} \cong \overline{EH}$ $\overline{DA} \cong \overline{HG}$ $\overline{AB} \cong \overline{GF}$
        $\overline{BC} \cong \overline{FE}$
        Quadrilateral CDAB $\cong$ EHGF
14. a. Yes   b. Yes
    c. All are congruent.
    d. Answers will vary
    e. Yes   f. A triangle
    g. Answers will vary. They should see a white chalice on a black background and two profiles in black on a white background.
    h. They are line segments.

Congruence: Area Activity (p. 37)
All answers are in square units.

1. 54	2. 48	3. 75
4. 96	5. 18	6. 25
7. 51	8. 27	9. 36

Convex and Concave Figures: Exercises (p. 40)
Drawings will vary. Examples are given.
1.

2.   3.

4.

Lines of Symmetry: Exercises (p. 43)
1. G = 0, E = 0, O = unlimited number, M = 1, E = 0, T = 1, R = 0, Y = 1 (If the Es are drawn carefully, they may have 1 line of symmetry each.)
3. No, unless the paper is square.
4. a. 3   b. 4   c. 5   d. 12
    e. 16
5. a.   c.
    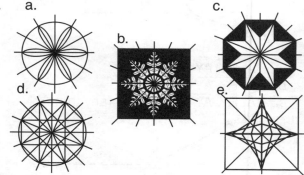
    b.
    d.   e.

Measurement of Angles (p. 44–45)
1.	a. 50°	b. 90°	c. 110°
	d. 130°	e. 40°	f. 80°
2.	a. 10°	b. 90°	c. 10°
	d. 110°	e. 61°	f. 45°
	g. 16°	h. 60°	i. 35°
	j. 109°	k. 170°	

Complementary and Supplementary Angles (p. 46)
3. $\angle 1$ and $\angle 2$, $\angle 1$ and $\angle 3$, $\angle 1$ and $\angle 4$, $\angle 2$ and $\angle 3$, $\angle 2$ and $\angle 4$, $\angle 3$ and $\angle 4$
4. $\angle 1$ and $\angle 5$, $\angle 3$ and $\angle 4$

Measurement of Angles: Exercises (p. 47–55)

1. a. scalene, isosceles, equilateral
    b. obtuse, acute, right
2. a. 180°
    b. The sum is 180°.
    c. The sum is 180°.
    d.

Angle	I	II	III	IV
∠A	66	69	42	43
∠B	46	37	48	107
∠C	68	74	90	30
Sum	180	180	180	180

   Answers may vary slightly due to inaccuracies in measurement, but all the sums should be 180°.
   The average is also 180°.
    e. 1) It equals 180°.
        2) m ∠A = 60°   m ∠B = 60°
           m ∠1 = 60°   m ∠3 = 60°
        3) They are congruent.
        4) They are congruent.
        5) The sums are equal.
3. a. 60°   b. 60°   c. 60°
    d. They are congruent.
4. a. 71°   b. 71°   c. 38°
    d. They are congruent.
5. a. 2.25 in.   b. 1.875 in.
    c. 1.5 in.
    d. 83°   e. 55°   f. 42°
    g. The longest side is opposite the largest angle, and the shortest side is opposite the smallest angle.

6.

# of Sides	# of Ang.	# of Diag.	# of Tri.	∠Sum of 1 Tri.	∠Sum of Poly.	m∠
3	3	0	1	180°	180°	60°
4	4	1	2	180°	360°	90°
5	5	2	3	180°	540°	108°
6	6	3	4	180°	720°	120°
7	7	4	5	180°	900°	128.57°
8	8	5	6	180°	1080°	135°
10	10	7	8	180°	1440°	140°
12	12	9	10	180°	1800°	150°
n	n	n - 3	n - 2	180°	(n - 2)180°	$\frac{(n-2)180°}{n}$

    a. The number of diagonals is three less than the number of sides.
    b. The number of triangles is two less than the number of sides.
    c. 180°

    d. It is found by subtracting two from the number of sides and multiplying times 180.
7. a. 70°   b. 70°   c. 70°
    d. 70°   e. 110°   f. 110°
    g. 110°   h. 110°
    i. ∠1, ∠2, ∠3, ∠4
        ∠5, ∠6, ∠7, ∠8
    j. Teacher check.
    k. 180°   l. 180°
    m. They are supplementary angles, which total 180°.
8. a. 90°   b. Yes   c. Yes
    d. Yes
9. a. 36°   b. 36°   c. 144°
    d. 144°   e. They are congruent.
10. a. 60°   b. 60°   c. 120°
11. a.

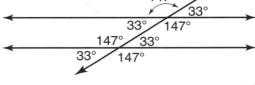

    b.

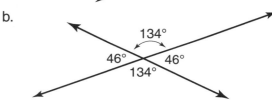

    c.

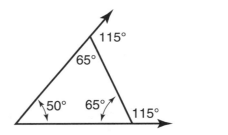

Constructions (p. 56)
The line segments are all the radii of the circles.

Constructions: Intersection Exercises (p. 57)

Points of intersection may be labeled with any letters.

1.   a.   b.   c.

   d.   e.   f.

   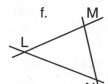

   g.   h.

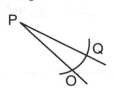   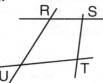

   i.   j.   k.

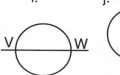

2.   a.   b.   c.

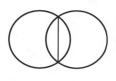

A. Construct a Line Segment Congruent to a Given Segment (p. 58)

Teacher check.

B. Bisect a Line Segment (p. 59)

1.   Yes
2.   a.   They are the same distance.
     b.   Yes
3.   Yes
4–5b.   Teacher check
5.   c.   Yes
     d.   Yes
     e.   Teacher check

C. Construct a Ray Perpendicular to a Line at a Given Point in the Line (p. 60–61)

1.   Yes
2–3.   Teacher check.

D. Construct a Perpendicular From a Point to a Line (p. 62–63)

1.   Yes
2–4.   Teacher check.

E. Bisect a Given Angle (p. 64)

1–2.   Teacher check.

F. Construct an Angle Congruent to a Given Angle (p. 65)

1–2.   Teacher check.

G. Construct a Triangle Congruent to a Given Triangle (p. 66)

Teacher check.

I. Construct a Line Parallel to a Given Line and at a Given Distance From It (p. 68)

Teacher check diagram.
1.   60°, 60°, 120°, 120°
2.   All four angles are 90°
3.   60°, 60°, 120°, 120°
4.   30°, 30°, 150°, 150°

J. Separate a Circle Into Six Congruent Arcs (p. 69)

Teacher check. Answers will vary.

Constructions: Exercises (p. 70–76)

1.   equilateral
     Teacher check triangle.
2.   isosceles
     Teacher check triangle.
3.   Teacher check triangles.
     a.   Yes
     b.   Yes
     c.   Triangles with congruent sides are congruent.
4.   Teacher check triangles.
     a.   Yes
     b.   Yes
     c.   Triangles with the same angle that have congruent sides to this angle are congruent.

5. Teacher check triangles.
    a. Yes
    b. Yes
    c. Triangles with two congruent angles and sharing congruent sides are congruent.
6. Teacher check square.
7. Teacher check rectangle.
8. a. 4 in.
    b. 2 in.
    c. 5 in.
9. a. 10 cm
    b. 7 cm
    c. 9 cm
10. Teacher check line segment.
11. Teacher check line segment and triangle.
12. a–e. Teacher check.
    f. It is a right angle.
13. a–d. Teacher check.
    e. It lies on line XZ.

Geometric Patterns and Addition (p. 78)
Teacher check arrays.

Paper Folding (p. 82–83)
1–5. Teacher check
6. Teacher check folds. Answers will vary.
7. Teacher check folds.
    a. Answers will vary. The folds form a triangle.
    b. They are congruent.
    c. They are congruent.
    d. It is a parallelogram.
8. a–c. The bisectors/altitudes all intersect.

Prisms (p. 86)
1. rectangle
2. triangle
3. Yes
4. Yes

Patterns for Prisms:
Triangular Prism (p. 88)
1. a. 2, 3
    b. 6
    c. 9
Rectangular Prism (p. 89)
2. 6, 12, 8

Pentagonal Prism (p. 90)
3. a. 2, 5, 7
    b. 10, 15

Prisms Table (p. 91)
4. a. Triangular Regions, 6, 9, 5
    b. Quadrilateral Regions, 8, 12, 6
    c. Pentagonal Regions, 10, 15, 7
    d. Hexagonal Regions, 12, 18, 8

Pyramids (p. 93)
4. 5, 5, 8 (This includes the base.)

Pyramid Table (p. 94)
5. a. Triangular Region, 4, 6, 4
    b. Quadrilateral Region, 5, 8, 5
    c. Pentagonal Region, 6, 10, 6
    d. Hexagonal Region, 7, 12, 7

Spheres (p. 97)
1. a circle
2. a. a circle
    b. a circle
    c. a circle
    d. unlimited
    e. unlimited
    f. It is the intersection of the cuts that divide the orange in half.

Volumes and Surface Areas: Exercises (p. 106–107)
1. Triangular Prism:
    Volume = 288 cm^3
    Surface Area = 336 cm^2
    Triangular Pyramid:
    Volume = 96 cm^3
    Surface Area = 192 cm^2
2. Cylinder:
    Volume = 904.78 in.^{3}
    Surface Area = 552.92 in.^{2}
    Cone:
    Volume = 301.59 in.^{3}
    Surface Area = 326.73 in.^{2}
3. Sphere:
    Volume = 65,449.85 ft.^{3}
    Surface Area = 7,853.98 ft.^{2}

4. Pentagon:
    Area = 6.88 in.^{2}
  Pentagonal Prism:
    Volume = 41.28 in.^{3}
    Surface Area = 73.76 in.^{2}
  Pentagonal Pyramid:
    Volume = 13.76 in.^{3}
    Surface Area = 46.88 in.^{2}

Acknowledgement: The Illinois Department of Education